Building Blocks for Relationships

iUniverse books may be ordered through booksellers or by contacting:

iUniverse
1663 Liberty Drive
Bloomington, IN 47403
www.iuniverse.com
1-800-Authors (1-800-288-4677)

ISBN: 978-0-595-49156-8 (pbk)
ISBN: 978-0-595-61924-5(cloth)
ISBN: 978-0-595-60987-1 (ebk)

Printed in the United States of America

iUniverse rev 12/08/2008

Dedication

This book is about establishing relationships according to Bible precepts. Many years ago, my concept of relationship did not extend beyond what I could get for myself in my transactions with others. If you are hearing this for the first time, you might think that I was normal. I may have been normal, but I was far from realizing the Father's will for relationships in my life. My sense of relationship was very skewed and self-centered. Then I met a woman I wanted to spend my life with. Her sense of relationship, marriage, family, and commitment were foreign to me, yet intriguing. As we both grew in the Lord, her ways became more apparent and clearer to me as I came to understand her purpose in light of the living Word. Her connection to me changed my perspective on relationships and gave me new life as we continued together to learn more of God's ways day-by-day.

Today, she is my wife and has been the completer and life partner who continues to teach me more about relating to her and relating to others through Christ. I dedicate this book to my wife, Terry, who has been a source of total support and my cheerleader in everything and anything I choose to do, especially in writing this book.

Contents

Acknowledgments

I want to thank the people who have made this book possible. There are too many to mention, but each one encouraged me in some way to write this book. The most prominent are the teachers of God's Word who have over the years consistently guided me to new and greater understanding. Without their teachings, this book would not have been possible.

Specifically, I want to thank Reverend Vincent Finnegan, who for over the past two decades has been a spiritual leader to me, my family and my many friends throughout New York state and elsewhere. His teachings have been an inspiration that have led me to study the Word more intently. Reverend John McCave is my other inspiration and a good friend. Through his works and teachings, I have been inspired to search the Bible for deeper understanding and to be assured that biblical principles I have taught accurately line up with the Word. Another good friend and pastor to whom I owe much gratitude is Reverend Glenn Post, who was my shepherd, mentor and friend for many years and the man of God who presided over my ordination. To these men, I am eternally grateful and look forward to an eternity of fellowship to come.

My single biggest inspiration for this book and the person who has given me the most encouragement is my daughter, Jillann Gonzalez, who has been my technical advisor, editor, and moral supporter. While proofreading, she would often pause and apply or question herself about the precepts in her own life. Her feedback was substantial and a great help. I want to thank Jill for her critical contributions

1

and especially for reading the manuscript many times over, the last time for grammar and conformity. A book such as this is written to give instruction on how to apply concepts that are new to us, and it requires many bullet points, indentations, and text boxes that present a number of opportunities for inconsistency. To a large degree, Jill has taken over that dreaded responsibility and has done a remarkable job with it. I am ever so thankful for Jill and all her assistance.

This work is in great part a result of seminars conducted for members of our church, Church of Divine Grace, and other friends. The teachings on relationships originated from marriage and family counseling and group teachings. I want to thank all those who participated in these teachings, both church members and friends who these teachings were originally prepared for.

Finally, I want to thank my family for allowing me the time during evenings and weekends to work and finish the manuscript. For my dear wife, Terry, and for my darling daughter, Dolores, I realize it was a sacrifice in order that I could have such gain. Their love and understanding goes beyond what words can describe.

Introduction

A role model is a person who exemplifies the behavioral characteristics, lifestyle, and social or economic status that one admires and chooses to emulate. I would like you to take a moment and reflect on the people you have looked up to as role models. Consider the qualities or circumstances that persuaded you to want to be like them. Now, if you would, eliminate all but the one person you think had the most impact on your life.

Who has served as your role model?

My _____ has served as my role model!

Have you imitated that role model in every way?

I ____ (have, have not) imitated my role model in every way.

It is very likely that you have not had a perfect role model to imitate in every way. People by nature are each flawed and imperfect in one way or another. Someone may be your role model in a limited way, but no one that you know is the perfect role model. We are given only one example of a perfect role model, and that is the Messiah, Jesus Christ whose example each and every one of us can follow. Christ was the apostle Paul's example, and we can look to Paul as a prototypical role model in his relationships with others to the extent he modeled his behavior after Christ. Paul says in 1 Corinthians 4:16:

Wherefore I beseech you, be ye followers of me. (KJV)

In the KJV you are called out to follow after the apostle Paul. If you examine this closer, in the NASB version you see that to follow is explained as living according to the Gospel, which can be accomplished by imitating the example of how to live one's life as seen in the life of the apostle Paul. We know that the example in the gospel that Paul followed is provided by the Lord Jesus Christ.

Therefore I exhort you, be imitators of me. (NASB)

The apostle Paul tells the Church to "follow my example." His example is based on the teachings of Jesus according to the revealed Word of God. There are many people who can serve as good role models in limited ways, but only a few people can lead us in the steps of Jesus Christ. For the most part, we must go at it alone, stumbling through life in the steps of those who, in their limited way, exhibit righteous qualities. However, we must remain in the ready to disclaim their leadership when they stray off the righteous path.

We have only one perfect example, our Lord Jesus Christ. We need to arrive in our lives at the point that we can look only to Him and crave to imitate Him in every way. We must work to rise to a patterning of our lives to be like Jesus.

Our study is about building up relationships. There have been many books written and seminars conducted that discuss building relationships, but most are not told from a Christian point of view. Other works as well, written for Christians in churches throughout the land have fallen short of the mark. Some of these works are excellent and, if the teachings are applied properly, can yield positive results. We are not going to discuss these how-to secular methods, but instead, we will turn to the Bible to learn what it says regarding relationships. Then we will study the qualities that are found in the best example of a relationship, Jesus and the Father. We will explore the foundation principles Jesus used to build relationships with others while He was here on earth. We can agree that His principles worked perfectly for Him, and you will want to understand how these principles are sure to work just as well for you.

The primary relationship we want to consider is the one between Jesus and the Father. Didn't they have the right, perfect relationship? Let us review some elements of their relationship:

They did not lie to one another. (John 17:17)

Each held nothing back from the other, [except for the time of the end of the world God reserved for Him only to know]. But of that day and hour knoweth no *man*, no, not the angels of heaven, but My Father only. (Matthew 24:36)

They had full trust in each other, but were willing to yield to the other's judgment. (Luke 22:42)

Their love was, is, and will be inseparable. (John 17:26)

Isn't this the type of relationship you yearn to have? God offers each of us the opportunity to have similar relationships with others as He has with Jesus. In order for you to have God's type of relationship you must first have a quality relationship with God. Then, you must establish a relationship of quality with Jesus, and subsequently you may have quality relationships with others. Whether or not you have a good relationship is strictly up to you. You can have a perfect relationship with Jesus, and you can have a perfect relationship with others you invite to partake in your life.

John 15:13

**Greater love hath no man than this,
that a man lay down his life
for his friends.**

Throughout our study, unless otherwise noted, we will utilize the Authorized King James Version of the Bible (KJV) as the source for scripture references. We will also review scripture in other versions where the KJV is not substantially clear to bring forth the full modern understanding of the scripture.

In this book, you will learn about the basic elements that are fundamental to every relationship. The main source we will utilize for exploring relationships is the Holy Scriptures that can be found only in the Bible, the inimitable Word of God. We will establish a set of biblical principles for relationships found in the Bible, which I've called "Higher Ground Principles."

As Christians we have been called to live out our lives in imitation of the Lord Jesus, according to Christian principles. Therefore, we are obligated to know these principles and to embrace them as the pattern source for our behavior as we relate to others. This can only be accomplished by applying biblical principles in the course of daily living. We cannot simply be Christian on Sunday mornings and something else the remainder of the week. Our lifestyles, in their totality, must conform to the lifestyle of the Gospel, even if it requires radical change. As we adapt our lifestyles to Christian principles, our lives will change. How we view others, and more importantly, how we treat and deal with others, will transform into a pleasant and enjoyable experience each and every time.

The second part of the book continues the exploration of "Qualities for Christian Living" by examining various critical categories of the Christian's life that pose severe challenges to establishing and sustaining sound relationships. These challenges include the "how-to" on handling conflict with others, offenses you are prone to commit and offenses committed against you, and handling conflict within the church. We will examine what the Word teaches on how your perspective on money impacts your personal financial condition and affects relationships with others.

We will consider the effect of spiritual laws, how they always work the same for everyone who meets their conditions. You don't have to be a Christian to enjoy the effect of a spiritual law. Spiritual laws like physical and natural laws have existed since creation. God has handed down detailed explanations to His people throughout time, as seen in the Law of Moses to the Israelites and subsequently throughout the scriptures. These laws work the same all the time for everyone. You can liken it to rain: when it rains, it rains on everyone. The promises of God are spiritual. Certain promises made to Abraham were made while he was yet a Gentile. Abraham is God's designee to be the father of nations two generations before Jacob was born, before the nation Israel was chosen as God's people. "Abraham believed God, and it was accounted to him for righteousness" (Romans 4:3). Likewise, every one who believes God will also receive God's promises. *Building Blocks for Relationships* displays godly principles that work equally for the Christian and the non-Christian when applied. My hope is that you will try these principles and apply them in your daily life and, whether Christian or not, enjoy a richer life and a higher quality in your relationships. I trust you to work on having a perfect relationship in your life.

Our study concludes with a review of what constitutes a perfect relationship. It leads us into a deeper understanding of how love and forgiveness are the main support for a healthy and vibrant relationship with the ones you choose to spend your life with.

While reading this book, you will find it helpful to keep a Bible by your side. Bible quotes appear often, and to amplify your understanding, you should go directly to the scripture and harvest for yourself the wonderful truths that it unveils. I prefer the King James Version for myself, but you are free to use the version that you are most familiar with. My encouragement is for you to use the Bible in conjunction with your reading.

The design of this work allows for individual reading or for group teaching for any number of participants. If you would like assistance in how to organize and conduct the teaching or to prepare for an event for your family, fellowship, Bible study group or church, please feel free to contact me, and I will assist you in preparing for the event. I only ask that you read the book in its entirety before you undertake the responsibility of teaching it to others. May God bless you abundantly, in Christ.

Gaspar

I. Laying the Foundation

Building Blocks for Relationships is a study of the principles in the Bible that set the foundations for all relationships. These principles guide you to build up and encourage virtuosity, love, and care in handling your affairs, in your manner of dealing with others, and in pursuing the purposes that bring and bind you together with someone else. Our study is based on biblical principles. Since the principles for building relationships are based on spiritual laws, when you do as is commanded in the Bible, you receive the intended benefit. This occurs even when you do not believe that the Bible is God's Word revealed to man. In this study, we will examine the scriptures for greater understanding of biblical principles with the expectation that when applied they will actually work.

The biblical field of study on relationships is very broad. While this study and workshop touches on the fundamentals that you are likely to apply in a relationship, it does not by any means exhaust the topic. As you begin your new self-assessment of how you relate to others, bear in mind that this, at best, is a work in progress. Likewise, building up your relationship will take much work and will require consistent effort to enable you to claim even the slightest mastery of skill in relationship building.

The book of Ecclesiastes teaches on the preference for man to have relationships. Either we cooperate together to build on a successful endeavor, or we compete to outdo each other. The advantage clearly falls to the side of cooperation (Ecclesiastes 4:9–13).

> I have seen that every labor and every skill which is done *is the result of* rivalry between a man and his neighbor. This too is vanity and striving after wind. (Ecclesiastes 4:4; NASB)

While it takes at least two people to establish a relationship, the only one you can absolutely exercise control over is yourself. A relationship is not built on controlling the actions of others, but on the degree and ability you possess over your own self, which is self-control.

Self-control is the sole guide to adhere to. Most of us practice control over other people. That will lead to conflict, frustration, and, if there is anything worse, we will experience that as well. We must begin by breaking the cycle of wanting to control others, and we must start to exercise self-control. This will instantly improve our relationships and increase the potential for better relationships in the future.

Our study will not equip you with the secular skills and techniques for maintaining a relationship. Surely, there is a place for their application as well. However, this study focuses on building the biblical foundations for the construct of a godly relationship. Let us begin by understanding that according to God's Word (1 Corinthians 4:4-5) we are forbidden to judge others. You should not stand in judgment of another's level of spirituality or the amount of Word knowledge your partner may or may not have. Instead, concentrate on your own abilities so that you may rise up to be the spiritual leader and lead by example in building up your relationship. This will require much sacrifice on your part, (the sacrifice of restraining yourself) and you should be prepared to sacrifice everything to maintain the biblical precepts required in a godly relationship.

II. Have T.H.I.S. in Your Relationship

Higher Ground Principle # 1

Establish relationships on the principles taught in the Bible.

To fulfill its purpose, a relationship must be healthy, prosperous, and robust. It must be regularly groomed and fed with proper nutrition to prevent sickness, disease, and death. The base elements of the foundation for a healthy relationship are Truth, Honesty, Integrity, and Sincerity (THIS).

Truth

Truth is correct knowledge or doctrine. It is the lowest common denominator for knowledge or information, whose material substance cannot be changed.

Truth is fidelity (the quality or state of being faithful), constancy (freedom from change).

A truth is always the same and works the same all the time, every time, without exception. For example, gravity is a truth. Whenever an object is dropped, it will always fall to the ground. No matter how many times you try this, it will always work the same way. This is known as a law of physics *(physical laws)*. There are laws of nature *(natural laws)* that yield a specified result when certain conditions are met, such as planting a seed in order for it to grow into a plant. There are also laws of men *(man-made laws)* that are generally weak and inconsistent, because they are subjective and governed by varying circumstances and emotional persuasions.

There are also spiritual truths, or principles in the Bible, that act as *spiritual laws*. When applied, these truths consistently produce a predictable result. These spiritual laws are put into operation when we act upon what we believe, or better said, when we act on our faith. "A soft answer turneth away wrath" (Proverbs 15:1). It works every time.

Knowing and believing that Jesus is the Son of God makes you free from dogmas and untrue worship. Jesus is the way, and He always leads us to the truth via the true worship of God. Others that we might follow lack the quality of absolute truth and can and will lead us away from true worship. There is deceitfulness from others, institutions, and governments, and there is deceitfulness that comes from within oneself. The hardest to overcome, of course, is self-deceit. Self- deceit leads us away from true worship of God into worshipping other things with the expectation that these other things will do for us what God promises, is willing and is able to do. Self deceit is among the biggest un-truths that plague mankind and that affects our basic relationship with God, and consequently affects our relationship with others.

Who changed the truth of God into a lie, and worshipped and served the creature more than the Creator, who is blessed for ever. Amen. (Romans 1:25)

Changing the truth, which is a euphemism for lying, causes encasement and imprisonment, and removes freedom from our daily lives. We become encased, and our hearts become encrusted. This is a spiritual law at work. This is why you feel so bad and uneasy after telling a lie. Lying leaves us heavily laden with guilt brought about by sin.

> Therefore thou art inexcusable, O man, whosoever thou art that judgest: for wherein thou judgest another, thou condemnest thyself; for thou that judgest doest the same things. But we are sure that *the judgment of God is according to truth* against them which commit such things. (Romans 2:1–22)
>
> Charity [which is *love*] suffereth long, and is kind; charity envieth not; charity vaunteth not itself, is not

puffed up, Doth not behave itself unseemly, seeketh not her own, is not easily provoked, thinketh no evil; Rejoiceth not in iniquity, but *rejoiceth in the truth.* (1 Corinthians 13:4–6)

Love rejoices in the truth. Living in truth keeps us filled with joy and leaves no room for remorse.

If you want joy in your relationship, then you should build the relationship on truth. You may desire to improve your relationship, and this will take some effort and hard work on your part. To begin a new relationship or to rejuvenate a decaying one, you must reveal and live the truth. You should do a self-assessment of what you've yet to completely reveal. Then, gird up your loins and have a heart-to-heart conversation with your partner. God defines truth in Jesus, and Jesus is your best role model for building a relationship on truth. Remember that men should not judge one another, because we are each guilty of the same things. You will find that as you come together around the truth, it will diminish the passion to judge one another.

Truth without judgment sets us free and is the fountain of rejoicing that waters the relationship. We find truth in the Messiah, Jesus Christ.

Honesty
Higher Ground Principle # 2

Have honest behavior and integrity, and be sincere in everything you do.

Now that we have discussed truth, let's look at another foundation to a sound and healthy relationship: honesty.

Honesty is fairness and straightforwardness of conduct dealing in truth. (Exodus 23:1–9)

Honesty is best defined as always being truthful. Honesty is essential to building up a relationship, but it is often used as a tool for measuring what is said. Honesty applies to things said, and by extension, it applies to behavior as well. "Actions speak louder than words" is a very popular saying, and it carries a lot of weight. A person may speak words that are true, but their actions, gestures, posture, and facial expression may convey meaning incongruous with the message. This is deceptive and dishonest since it's not representative of the truth in its entirety.

In the work environment, for example, a married woman might have a conversation with a male co-worker who invited her out for drinks. She may say, "I'm married," in a manner that encourages continuing the conversation. Perhaps she gives a look or positions her body in an inviting way that conflicts with her statement of unavailability. Although she told the truth about being married, she failed to be honest.

An honest relationship has boundaries that are clear and discernable. When starting a relationship, these boundaries must be established. In an honest relationship, the extent of the relationship is well defined and distinctly classified. The conversation between the co-workers should spell out that they can be friends, and if they meet after work for social purposes, they should be joined by their spouses. The relationship is defined as a friendship, and classified as how they will relate to each other.

In the relationship, you are not to address one another in any misleading or dishonest way. Honesty leads us to godliness and is Godlike in every way. Honesty has no variableness, is always consistent, and engenders an atmosphere of reliability in each other If our intentions are honest from the beginning we would extricate ourselves from situations where we are provoked by lust or covetousness. In so doing we deny "ungodliness and worldly lusts" and elect to live soberly. (Titus 2:11–12). When we are consistently honest, we inspire confidence from those around us and especially from our partners. Your partner, mate, spouse, child, friend, or employee can take refuge in knowing that a predictable and safe environment will exist when dealing with you. You, on the other hand, will experience openness, truth, great peace and joy with the ones you choose to be with.

Honesty builds trust. A good example of this trust is found in 2 Kings 12:15. I will quote from the NASB because the language in this verse of scripture is made so much clearer to our understanding.

> Moreover, they did not require an accounting from the men into whose hand they gave the money to pay to those who did the work, for they dealt faithfully.

The men administering the funds to pay the laborers repairing the temple received donations and contributions, but no one felt it necessary to keep or require any accounting from them because they were honest and well renowned throughout their community for their honesty. No one would doubt that they did exactly what was required and what was expected of them. Honesty goes a long way in any relationship by removing burdens of guilt or doubt.

Honesty is fundamental to strengthening your relationship. When you deal honestly with your partner, there will be no aura of doubt or slack in trust. Your actions and your judgments will be acceptable all the time. Your partner is assured that your motives or purposes are derived from honest intentions, since they have known you only to be honest at all times.

Integrity

As we increase our appreciation for the foundational principles of truth and honesty, our minds expand to receive and understand the principle of integrity and how it should be applied to our relationships.

Like truth and honesty, integrity is essential to building a solid foundation for your relationships to rest upon in the years to come. Unlike truth and honesty, integrity provides the assurance that a partner can be relied upon to uphold the godly principles beneficial to the relationship. One is assured that the other party in the relationship will perform the righteous duties required, and if one party needs correction, the other is there to stand firm to assure that truth and honesty are upheld.

Integrity is the state of being complete or undivided, exercising righteousness without wavering.

I will *behave myself wisely in a perfect way*. O when wilt thou come unto me? I will walk *within my house with a perfect heart*. I will set *no wicked thing before mine eyes:* I hate the work of them that turn aside; it shall not cleave to me. (Psalms 101:2–3)

Integrity is the manifestation of wise behavior that originates in your heart, the part of your mind that is the seat of your convictions. A person of integrity understands the principles in God's Word and does not waiver from them in the slightest way. It is easy to yield to your fleshly desires, which as the Word tells us are always in opposition to God's ways. In order to resist such temptations, you must have prepared yourself in advance by incorporating a sense of passive resistance. Let's say a family member has a tendency to say or do things that really irk you. Now, you can wait until they come at you again and react accordingly, or you can prepare yourself to resist the temptation to respond in kind. You will uphold your integrity by keeping to the biblical principles, such as loving your enemy, even though he is not literally your enemy, but at the moment, your feelings could cause you to treat him like one.

We find that integrity is founded on four principles:

1.   Wisely chosen behavior that is accepted by others.

2.   Having purity about your ways, beginning and emanating at home, but carried out throughout your walk and conversations as a mark for others to see.

3.   Not seeking or finding pleasure in ungodly and wicked behavior, nor engaging in impure things, no matter how politically correct they may seem or how many others are behaving in that ungodly way.

4.   Not allowing the ungodly works of others to enter or stay in your mind, and not harboring destructive images or thoughts in your mind, but instead, being empty of these thoughts and remaining open to the Lord with a clean mind.

In your relationships, integrity will be more abstract than truth and honesty. Truth can be easily discerned, and if you get away with a lie, it may not be long before the truth comes out. Honesty is immediately noticeable in your behavior, and guilt will haunt the believer when he or she has been dishonest. Most likely, your partner will know that you were not acting honestly. However, lack of integrity leaves room for doubt and time for the culprit to come up with a novel explanation. Your partner may get a whiff that something is not quite up to snuff, but usually has to file it away for future examination. At this point, you will be under their watch and likely to get caught at the next slipup.

Many friendships, marriages and other relationships are destroyed for lack of integrity on one or both partners' part. These instances of unspoken issues are the substance of what future disagreements are sparked by, when an unspoken issue later becomes the center of debate during a mutual disagreement. Women, in general, have a higher or keener awareness of this phenomenon, and men usually complain that women always bring up the past in a fight. This may seem unfair to the person being accused, but it's his or her lack of integrity that usually brings things to a boil.

The solution may seem simplistic, although to the culprit, it's very difficult to implement. The answer is to have integrity. To have integrity means that you are a truthful person and everything you do is of honest purpose and intent. Chapter 4 of the Book of Ephesians is highly instructional to the believer who wants to learn and practice biblical principals relevant to this topic. Ephesians 4:14 speaks to no longer being children tossed to and fro. Ephesians 4:15 directs us to speak the truth. The remainder of the chapter encourages change from what we are to becoming men and women of renewed minds. The latter part of the chapter from verses 21 to 32 reminds us that Jesus is our standard for truth, and it instructs us on some basics. It tells us to stop acting the way we used to act in our "old man" days which were "corrupt according to deceitful lusts". Integrity bears the charge to put away lying, to not harbor anger, to not take what is not yours. Entering into an illicit relationship is stealing from your spouse, and stealing from the other person's time and emotions that are ill placed. When reality strikes it will cause everyone connected to undergo severe recovery pains. Integrity also bears the charge not to speak words that tear others down. Instead of speaking corruptly about others, we are to speak only things that build others up, and to perform such other things as being kind, tenderhearted, and forgiving. Integrity will dwell in you when you have internalized these principles in the depth of your convictions, so that when confronted with an unsavory situation you will not think from an evil reference, but you will speak and deal from a godly reference.

If you want your relationship to flourish without strife and conflict, integrity is the element to work on in your life.

Sincerity

Sincerity is also abstract and difficult to identify in someone's behavior right away. You have to get to know a person in order to see that he is not always sincere. Sincerity in your behavior can be masked with varying degrees of disguise. You can do something that is seemingly good for your partner, but have the wrong intentions for doing so. Or you could say something that sounds nice, but it may not be something you mean. When sincerity is lacking, you get hypocrisy in one form or another. Remember what the Lord thought about the hypocrisy of the Pharisees. They pretended to be obedient to the Law of Moses, but only as far as what might be publicly seen. In private, they did whatever they pleased. Those Jews, the ones that were called hypocrites by the Lord, did not have a very good relationship with Jesus. In fact, John the Baptist referred to them as a generation of vipers. They were insincere and wished only that they be thought of as holy, but it was solely for the purpose of having things their way.

Ask yourself, "Is this what I do in my relationship? Do I give the appearance of doing God's Word, but I'm only pretending so that I appear as a just person?" This is an inherent problem with many relationships, and a problem that is often introduced into new relationships. It certainly merits your close attention to the issue of sincerity in your life.

Sincerity is the personal quality of living life from a pure motive without deceit; genuine.

> Now this is our boast: Our conscience testifies that we have *conducted ourselves* in the world, and especially in our relations with you, *in the holiness and sincerity that are from God.* We have done so not according to worldly wisdom but according to God's grace. (2 Corinthians 1:12; NIV)

Sincerity does not allow your thoughts toward or about others to be tainted with evil for personal gain or to deal hypocritically with someone else to gain popularity or maintain favor or friendship with others. Sincerity is always doing what is right, fair, and unquestionable. If you want to be sincere, begin with truth and honesty, and then, deliberately build integrity into every aspect of your life. As you engage with your partner, you will have no desire but to consistently do things that are motivated by genuine intentions and that will achieve godly purposes in your relationship. Your partner will know and trust your every action. In a relationship, integrity generates trustworthiness, because the parties will know that each one's actions are based on truth and for truth's sake.

When there has been an obvious breach in integrity it is incumbent upon the "villain" to promptly move to repair the breach and restore himself or herself with their partner. A relationship should be built on firm and solid foundations to withstand assaults on our relationships due to our human frailties that can lead us to default. Should a breach occur in your relationship you must move quickly to mend it, and the aggrieved partner must reach deep into their soul to find mercy, employ the love of God within them and activate brotherly love. This response will be encouraged by honest forth coming, and in how they handle immediate interaction to stem the emotional bleed. A breach of integrity must be remedied by immediate divulgence of the circumstances and causes that brought the situation about. Many relationships have been severely damaged from innocent behavior in a bad situation, or bad behavior in an innocent situation. The cause must be assessed and treated by both parties, and if needed a competent third party mediator should be involved.

Always in Remembrance (2 Peter 1:15)

1. Relationship pertains to our affairs and _____ with others.

2. We can exercise total _____ over our own actions.

3. Godly relationships are built on _____.

4. Truth is _____ knowledge or doctrine.

5. Laws describe things that _____ the same all the time: physical laws, natural laws, and spiritual laws. Man-made laws are weak because they are not founded on absolute _____.

6. Spiritual laws are operated by _____ and by actions corresponding to one's beliefs.

7. Truth shall make you free is a _____ law.

8. Any alteration of the truth is _____.

9. Only God can _____ in truth.

10. When we live in truth, our lives are full of _____.

11. Honesty is the product of one's conduct when dealing in _____.

12. Integrity is the state of being _____ and undivided in one's behavior.

13. Behavior that is of wise _____ is an aspect of integrity.

14. Purity in one's ways is an aspect of _____.

15. _____ is required when faced with temptation.

16.   *Not holding* _____ *thoughts in one's mind reflects integrity in one's character.*

17. *Living life with pure motives and without* _____ *is a quality of sincerity.*

18.   *Thoughts tainted with* _____ *or hypocrisy are not founded on sincerity.*

Scripture Reference:
Exodus 23:1–10; Psalms 101:2–3; 2 Corinthians 1:12; Titus 2:11–12; 2 Kings 12:15;   Ephesians 4:14

III. What Constitutes a Relationship?

Higher Ground Principle # 3

Identify the biblical qualities you want in your relationship.

A relationship is a state of affairs existing between those dealing with others.

A relationship exists between two or more persons who have a purpose in common such as, husband/wife, doctor/ patient, parent/ child, teacher/student, employer/employee, and friend/friend.

A relationship is entered for the good of the participants, partners, or associates who will benefit in a common or symbiotic interrelationship. The parties in a relationship can choose to cooperate by sharing information, partnering skills and talents, or agreeing to nurture and support one another. When motives are clear, the parties to the relationship may offer up their contribution without expecting an equal portion or value in return. Our modern culture emphasizes a fifty-fifty contribution from husband and wife and equal participation in the marriage. This is a faulty presumption that leads to much conflict and distress, as there are so many variables that cannot be measured or have their emotional impact accounted for in a marriage. This applies to other relationships. A homemaker and mother may not feel as important as the executive or professional husband enjoying his daily practice, but she cannot measure how important it is for her husband to know that she is caring for the home and children, which he would prefer not to entrust to anyone else. The basis for measuring the contribution and participation is skewed from the other's point of view. What value or worth do you bring to your relationship, and do you fully comprehend the value perceived by others in that relationship?

Homemakers obliged to stay home and raise the children while the husband goes to work have been severely hurt by either spouse straying into relationships outside their own, or due to one or the other simply being overworked. The working spouse provider may stray, but they too may be hurt to learn that the wife/mother at home has been distracted from providing the utmost care for the children and the home. Either or both of these problems can be made to go away by applying the concepts we have learned about THIS. You may take inventory of where you are in your relationship and why you are in that place, remembering that you can exercise control over yourself, but your partner has to be educated and led to the point you are at so that they may elect to exercise control over themselves. Consider the following questions and truthfully answer them in your heart. When you have formed your answers I strongly recommend that you discuss them openly with your partner.

What do you want out of your relationship?

What were you seeking when you decided to enter the relationship? For example, did you enter the relationship because you wanted to give love or because you craved to be loved?

Were your motives clear, and did you have an agreement as to how the value and worth of contributions to the relationship were to be measured?

In formulating your answers to the above questions you may want to consider the following points about relationships:

The basis on which you established the relationship dictates the acceptable terms and conditions for that relationship. Re-examine your purpose and the reason for being in the relationship.

A godly person enters a relationship with a clean heart and seeks to have a clean life in the relationship. The relationship must in some way glorify the Lord.

An unselfish relationship will be founded on THIS (Truth, Honesty, Integrity, and Sincerity).

The worldly person enters a relationship only for personal gain.

A selfish relationship is formed for personal satisfaction and personal gain.

Lusting after someone and building a relationship purely on physical, sexual desires is a formula for disaster and can cause one or both persons to be severely hurt.

In some special way, the person in your relationship is a reflection of you. (In Acts 5:1–11, Ananias and Sapphira, husband and wife, conspired in their relationship to lie to, deceive, and cheat God. They violated the spiritual law of truth. Either one could have prevented the other and saved both their lives.)

Entering a relationship for the wrong reasons will most likely cause the decay and death of the relationship. In the case of Ananias and Sapphira it cost them their lives. The purpose you choose to form a relationship should not detract from the future growth and health of the relationship. A relationship for an illicit purpose will conclude in failure, guilt, or worse.

For example, a relationship formed with your doctor to cheat the insurance company, your accountant to cheat the IRS, or another person for illicit sex are all departures from truth and ultimately contribute to the destruction of the relationship.

Adultery is very high on the list. It is selfish and issues out hurt to everyone affected, spouses, children, extended family, the church community, friends, and even the workplace.

Suggestions for Overcoming Past Experiences

Don't try to fix what went wrong in the past, but start to do what is right—today, right now—and continue to do the right thing from now on. Begin to live a superior quality of life in your relationship. In the next chapter, we will study five essential biblical precepts that are necessary to the success of your relationship. It is important for you that these principles be applied.

> And having in a readiness to revenge all disobedience,
> when your obedience is fulfilled. (Corinthians 10:6)

Always in Remembrance (2 Peter 1:15)

1. Dealings with _____ constitute the basis for a relationship.

2. Relationships exist between persons who have a _____ __ in common.

3. We should _____ our purpose before forming a relationship.

4. The _____ for forming a relationship may strongly influence terms and conditions that govern the relationship.

5. A godly person enters a relationship with a _____ heart.

6 Unselfish relationships are founded on THIS: _____, _____, _____, and _____.

7. A worldly person enters a relationship for personal _____.

8. You should work in the relationship to do what is biblically right starting _____.

9. A relationship for an illicit purpose will conclude in _____, guilt, or worse.

10. The terms and conditions of your relationship should reflect a _____ benefit.

Scripture Reference:
Acts 5:1–11; 2 Corinthians 10:6

Building Blocks for Relationships (The Five Ss)

Higher Ground Principle # 4

Work your relationship for success.

What causes a relationship to work? The five Ss.

There may be a benefit to studying failed or decaying relationships to conclude why they failed. This would be a clinical approach, but it would not be novel. Our concern should not be why a relationship failed, but rather how a relationship is built up.

Let me introduce you to five fundamentals that will assure success in every relationship if they are applied. Each one of these is a spiritual principle Christ applied in his life to establish an everlasting relationship with you. Jesus gives us living examples in His daily walk and confirms them in His ultimate sacrifice. These principles each stands alone but together they complete the whole of the substance that drives the relationship and steers it in the proper course. If your relationship was a luxury car THIS would be the four wheels it stands on, and these five principles would be the inner workings that make it go; the transmission, engine and other working parts.

Sanctification: Set the parties aside or apart from the rest of the world at special moments and for special purposes. Keep your relationship personal and private, not public. Open the doors and allow in only those who support the success of your relationship.

> Wherefore Jesus also, that he might sanctify the people with his own blood, suffered without the gate. (Hebrews 13:12)

A relationship that is not sanctified (set apart) has its laundry aired everywhere. The wife shares with her friends stories of bedroom activities they have no business knowing about, the husband constantly complains to his friends of how bad a housekeeper his wife is, or that she is spendthrift, and so on. This should never be. What happens in the relationship stays in that relationship, unless there is imminent physical harm to be concerned about. If necessary both parties should seek and commit to obtaining professional help.

Exposing inner secrets to outsiders compounds the relationship further by two more errors. The first is a false sense that you have relieved your anxiety about the situation and are relieved by letting off steam about your partner, and the second is that you are dishing out well deserved justice on your partner by diminishing his image and tarnishing his reputation in the eyes of your friends. "My friends finally know who you really are", is the sense of self imposed justice you are walking away with. This makes you the better person, or so you'd like to think.

What truly occurs in this situation is that your friends now think rather poorly of your partner, and consequently, by extension they either pity you, or think that you're not too bright for having made such a poor choice, and then sticking with it throughout the ordeal. If it's about marriage, your friends would have you divorced and collecting alimony in no time. But relationships are more complicated than that. It is not that simple. What if you haven't told your partner what you think about him or her, or failed to mention how you felt about the particular situation you described to your friends? You told everyone else, but you haven't told him. Where does that leave you? In order to keep your relationship sanctified you must implement true and real solutions to the problems that arise. You must work at it together through "thick and thin" until a satisfactory solution is reached.

Sacrifice: Give up your preference so that the other person can have his or hers. This involves long suffering and patience. To suffer long is to take the hard times well and to trust that the chords that bind your relationship are strong enough to hold it together through difficult times.

> I am the good shepherd: the good shepherd giveth
> his life for the sheep. (John 10:11)

The attitude portrayed by Jesus is that He is willing to give up His life for His people. We see this also in King David that while he was yet a mere shepherd boy he faced a lion and then a bear armed only with his sling in order to protect his sheep. Jesus' people know they can trust Him, and Davis's sheep knew they could trust their shepherd to protect them against attacks. And so it must be between partners in a relationship, each confident as to where they stand and confident to know where their partner stands, and that they can trust one another to make sacrifices for each other. It is positive and affirming in the relationship when one or both are fully committed to sacrificing all that is necessary one for the other.

Let us not get so grave about this since you will probably never face a situation that you must sacrifice your life for your partner. There are many other sacrifices that can and should be made, and there are opportunities standing before you every day. To sacrifice is to give up something of value. Most of us have extreme value for our own opinions and for our pride. We'd rather die than give in when our mind is made up or we think a certain way. Here lies your greatest opportunity to begin to sacrifice for your partner. Don't fight for your position "till death do you part", but give way to your partner and sacrifice yourself not to have to prevail and unilaterally impose your will.

Substitution: Put yourself in your partner's place and understand his or her point of view. Can you allow this person to express a point of view without imposing your will, having to be right, or justifying yourself? Can't you just listen?

> For Christ also hath once suffered for sins, the just
> for the unjust, that he might bring us to God, being
> put to death in the flesh, but quickened by the Spirit:
> (1 Peter 3:18)

A substitution is taking the place for someone else. I would like to stress substitution in a very narrow sense of you putting yourself in your partner's place. This is ever more crucial in the wake of a disagreement, difference of opinion or an argument. Stop, pause and consider what your partner is trying to communicate. Put yourself in his or her place and bear the weight of their position as it pertains to you in this instance. You can do that by letting go of your immediate desire to be heard, to be right, and you substitute their position for yours.

Let us say two friends are discussing politics where one has very liberal views and the other has very conservative views, you are not being asked to agree with the other friend's point of view. You are being asked to place yourself in that position to understand how upsetting it is for others (especially a friend) not to understand your point of view. Once you get past the issue of the individual's right to have a divergent opinion, you will come to see that they did not necessarily expect agreement from you, that they merely want you to understand their point of view. In most instances both parties can walk away appeased or even justified in that their point of view was understood, although they couldn't convince one another to agree. When substitution is practiced the relationship is strengthened by mutual trust and respect for each other's point of view.

Submission: Give in to your partner's point of view. Acknowledge that he or she has a different perspective. Consider it not to be a better or worse idea than yours, simply different. Giving in is not surrendering.

> And he went a little further, and fell on his face, and prayed, saying, O my Father, if it be possible, let this cup pass from me: nevertheless not as I will, but as thou wilt. (Matthew 26:39)

Occasionally, your partner's point of view is going to make more sense than yours, although you still like your own point of view better. Sometimes it won't make as much sense as yours, but it's viable just the same. Once in a while we become deeply enmeshed in our own views and find it impossible to let go and accept someone else's view. When that situation comes up with your partner, if it's not detrimental, this is the time to submit. Let it go. After all, what's the difference between Chinese food and pizza if it's all about eating the food, anyway?

The most divisive moments in a relationship are centered about the inability of one party to submit to the other. When it comes to the order of Christian life, submission is a big problem. Submission should not be a problem to any of us since it is clearly defined in God's Word. "Wives submit to your own husbands", (Ephesians 5:22) is a source for many matrimonial disputes. We find little disagreement in that children are to submit to their parents and that pets are to submit to the kids. However, we so easily overlook (Ephesians 5:21) which calls us to "submit to one another in the fear of God". We can grasp that we are to submit to God and that we are to submit to every ordinance of man, but have the most difficult time in submitting to each other in love and for love's sake.

Survival: Persevere in the relationship through difficult times. The survival of a good and healthy relationship is vital, and a higher objective than persevering for yourself.

We are inclined to think of a relationship as pertaining to two people, and that is certainly not an incorrect way to regard a relationship. I would like to offer help with your view of a relationship, and step it up to a higher plane. Consider the aspects of a corporation, it can have one owner, two or many, but it is an entity of its own with perpetuity. A relationship is comprised of two people or more who have ownership in that relationship, but the relationship is an entity on to itself. You or your partner can and do exist outside of the relationship when you go about your other business, or perhaps engage in other, unrelated relationships. However, the relationship cannot exist without you. You each provide the substance that comprises the relationship. You bring the elements that make that relationship work, therefore, the higher the quality of your contribution the better the quality of the relationship, the entity itself. You have created a living entity (the relationship) which must be nurtured and supplied with its life essentials in order for it to survive. Survival of the relationship requires contribution on your part, and the more you contribute the more imminent its success.

> And there arose a great storm of wind, and the waves beat into the ship, so that it was now full. And he was in the hinder part of the ship, asleep on a pillow: and they awake him, and say unto him, Master, carest thou not that we perish? And he arose, and rebuked the wind, and said unto the sea, Peace, be still. And

the wind ceased, and there was a great calm. (Mark 4:37–39)

Knowing that they may lose their life as the boat takes in water and begins to sink, the disciples wake Jesus and accuse Him of not caring that they are about to perish. Throughout the ordeal, Jesus slept in the back of the boat. Human nature compels us to want others to suffer equally or worse than us. Imagine the men's anguish as they realized they were about to sink and Jesus was sleeping.

I cannot imagine that they awoke Him calmly with a gentle nudge or a soft call. These men were panic stricken, and they roused Jesus up with the same intensity of their anguish. If this were one of us, I am sure that our immediate response to a rude awakening would not be laced with kindness. But Jesus arose and instantly assessed the situation. He rebuked the wind and calmed the sea, and there was a great calm. Survival from the Lord's point of view was not to rail at the men for their discomposure and to yell back at them. Instead, He took positive and definitive action that calmed the entire situation and even calmed the men. Jesus did not try to make Himself righteous with the men. His actions caused a higher objective to be achieved in this situation.

Always in Remembrance (2 Peter 1:15)

1. _____ *sets the parties in the relationship apart from everyone else.*

2. *One should associate with persons who are in* _____ *of their godly relationship.*

3. _____ *is giving up your preference for the benefit of others in a relationship.*

4. *In the process of* _____, *you place yourself in your partner's position to better understand a divergent point of view.*

5. _____ *is not surrender, but an acknowledgement of a different perspective.*

6. *It is vital for a relationship to be healthy for its* _____.

Scripture Reference:
Hebrews 13:12; John 10:11; 1 Peter 3:18; Matthew 26:39; Mark 4:37-39; Ephesians 5:21-22

IV. Working to Build Up the Relationship

Higher Ground Principle # 5

Apply biblical principles in your relationship.

Know and apply spiritual laws.

It will be difficult to operate and apply what you don't know, so get busy learning. If you desire to grow in a skill or subject it is important to learn as much as possible about it before you put it into practice. Spiritual laws may at first seem distant and remote from your sphere of knowledge, but as you study them you will come to find they are not so remote or foreign. Spiritual laws are at work in every aspect of your life. They are written and taught throughout the Bible as principles of faith such that when applied consistently produce an intended result.

Love, respect, and submission are acts of the will. An act of the will means that you control when and how you exercise it by your own willingness to do it. These are also spiritual principles that yield spiritual fruit, more commonly known as godly effects on people. Love, respect, and submission are spiritual principles that when put into effect operate the spiritual law of reciprocity. "Therefore all things whatsoever ye would that men should do to you, do ye even so to them: for this is the law and the prophets". (Matthew 7:12) By doing to others as you would have them do unto you, a virtuous cycle is started that will soon yield the most positive interpersonal results. There are many more principles written throughout the Bible and you may want to build your own list to draw upon in time of need. I encourage you to search the scriptures and add other favorite spiritual principles and personalize your own list. (As a hint I suggest you start with Galatians 5:22–23, the fruit of the spirit.)

> Pray for us: for we trust we have a good conscience, in
> all things willing to live honestly. (Hebrews 13:18)

You can choose to love, respect, and submit to your partner for the common good of the relationship and when you do so, you must do it unconditionally, not expecting a reward and without holding a grudge. This describes a spiritual law for living life in "good conscience" and honestly in your relationship.

You can also choose to honor the role or authority of the other person in the relationship rather than to oppose it or contest it. This presumes that you are both clear as to what the roles to be fulfilled are and the extent to which each of you is charged with and committed to your respective role and responsibility. If roles and responsibilities are vague, unclear, or not agreed upon, they become a source for resentment and bitterness down the line. Likewise, authority and leadership must also be clear and distinct, and agreed upon if the relationship is to prosper by them and if you want conflict to be minimized.

Are the cues for handling your relationship taken from TV sitcoms? Sitcoms are the most damaging examples of standards to apply in your relationship. The cues the standards in your relationship should come from God's Word. So many relationships are entered into out of ignorance and ruled by the popular theme of the day. Celebrities are mistakenly set as the standard without taking into account the poor role models that they generally are when it comes to real life. Besides, you don't have the money to live the loose lifestyles that they do, and it takes longer for things to catch up with them than they will with you. Very few sitcoms last longer than a few seasons. God's Word lives and abides forever (1 Peter 1:23).

How do you present yourself in the relationship? Only you can choose the manner in which you will comport yourself in each and every relationship. A young woman may choose to act girlish with her boyfriend to appeal to him, perhaps because of her insecurity around him. Her lack of assurance leads her to determine that this is the best form of behavior. By choosing that behavior the young woman is casting herself into a role inviting a corresponding behavior from her boy friend that she may find condescending or insulting, if not today, then certainly later on in the relationship. Choose wisely how you present yourself in a relationship so that you elicit the type of treatment commensurate with your expectations and in line with how you desire to be treated.

Do you command respect by the responsible execution of duties in your role?

> Then Pharaoh sent and called Joseph, and they brought him hastily out of the dungeon: and he shaved himself, and changed his raiment, and came in unto Pharaoh. (Genesis 41:14)

Joseph's desire was to make the right first impression with Pharaoh that would establish a relationship of deep trust and confidence. This should be the model for how you present yourself in your relationships, always at your best.

In your present relationship you may notice that there are unacceptable patterns of behavior arising. These may come suddenly or may arise subtly as treatment toward one another shifts. When this occurs it is a symptom of malignant behavior that will eat away at the relationship like a cancer. A love filled scripture as the center for discussion may be the shortest route to a healthy cure among fellow believers, including a husband and wife. Great examples of practicable scriptures for these instances are: (Ephesians 5:25 – for husbands acting unlovingly towards their wives; Galatians 5:13 – "by love serve one another", in the case of one acting selfishly). Scripture must not be used to beat someone down or to shame them, but at the onset of the conversation to set the standard of how God's Word instructs us. If your partner refuses to accept the scripture, pray for them fervently and seek help.

What is the position that you hold in your relationship, and what is the manner in which you present yourself and carry out the duties and responsibilities of your position? How did the relationship start, and does it now need correction? These extremely relevant questions may not have easy answers. In that case discuss the future of your relationship. Start by identifying the near term and achievable goals important to the relationship. Then agree to work together toward the goal and divide the tasks accordingly. You may discover that once you both are on board with the first set of tasks it will become easier to tackle the next. A positive energy will exude and wonderful ideas will flow from the two of you together. Issues to consider in the framing of your new horizon are:

What are the relevant positions held or appointed in the relationship and who should bear responsibility?

How do you make yourselves accountable to each other?

Who is the leader or head? (Is one needed, and if so, is He or she acknowledged by the other?

What are the necessary functions and responsibilities in the relationship?

What aspects are unnecessary, or superfluous, and undesirable in the relationship? (i.e.; What do you not want your relationship to look like or to be like?)

Always in Remembrance (2 Peter 1:15)

*1. To _____ up my relationship, I should know and apply
spiritual laws.*

2. Love, respect, and submission are examples of acts of the _____.

*3. You should unconditionally love, submit, and respect the other for
the _____ good of the relationship.*

*4. You can choose to_____ the role and authority of
others.*

*5. Leadership and authority must be clear and distinct to avoid
_____.*

*6. Sitcoms and other popular sources are _____ examples of
social standards.*

*7. Do you command or do you demand _____ in
your relationship?*

*8. The _____ first impression establishes trust and confidence
in your relationship.*

Scripture Reference:
Galatians 5:22–23; Hebrews 13:18; 1 Peter 1:23; Genesis 41:14

V. Examining Faults in the Relationship

Higher Ground Principle # 6

Minimize the potential for failure in your relationship.

We don't want to dwell on failure for too long, but we must take a short side trip to help us determine the factors that need to incur change or that need radical surgery performed to enable a dysfunctional relationship and to prepare it to be built up.

Has the relationship entered into a vicious cycle?

A key symptom that tells if your relationship is on the ropes is that every day you allow yourself to say ever increasing and harsher things to your partner, or vise-versa. You become increasingly more callous toward one another and your attitude is less caring every day.

When does the relationship become not worth saving? If there is willingness, the relationship is worth saving. You've heard it said that "the grass is greener on the other side" or that "there are plenty of fish in the sea". I will not debate the veracity of either of those colloquialisms, but I will make the case that relationships may have multiple complications and may affect many innocent people when they go sour. If you desire to present yourself in purity to the Lord then you cannot have weighty baggage holding you down. You should desire to give your utmost to make your relationship work in a godly way.

Have you gone to the point of no return? Is the behavior of either one reprobate? This could be true if you act as though you hate each other and there is no willingness to compromise or change. See (Titus 1:15–16).

Has the relationship become the venue for dishonoring events between you and your partner?

Do you feel that you are the butt of your partner's bad jokes, that you are often caused to bear insults or made to feel inferior at social gatherings, and that communication is mostly one-way and often condescending?

Is it an intellectual or an emotional relationship? Emotional relationships are comprised of outbursts and outrageous behavior. This characteristic is depicted in a movie scene where the wife is destructively hurling dishes about in a fit of anger at her husband. Although generally short-lived these outbursts can be the source of escalation leading to abusive language or even physical violence. The effect of emotional outbursts cannot be projected before hand, but they can be very costly in both dollars and emotional capital of the relationship. Forgiveness on the part of the parties is hard to come by and the event is definitely going to leave a scar. Prepare yourself mentally to avoid blow outs, and if you encounter difficulty in achieving this, consider that a medical exam would be prudent to identify hormonal or chemical imbalances that need treatment by a qualified physician. Women undergoing menopause should have this in check, and we should each take care to minimize confrontations when one or both are stressed. Intellectual relationships are too guarded; little is communicated with honesty. This characteristic is mostly ruled by silence or unrelated topics dominating the conversations between you. These conversations are polite but avoid or skirt around the issues at hand. One may prefer to dwell at this level to maintain a comfortable place and not deal with the harshness of other things. Men are more likely to employ this tactic defensively for fear of being drawn into a fight they are ill prepared to engage in, and one they are certain they cannot win. The truth in this case is somewhat evident and both parties by silent agreement consent not to deal with it, at least for the time being. The effects here are long lasting and forgiveness rarely comes in time to bail the relationship out. These are the elements that comprise the hidden reasons why in a marriage one spouse wants a divorce. Intellectual relationships should be avoided from ruling your life, and you should start taking measures to deal with this aspect right away. The longer you wait to handle the matter, the more complicated and abstract the facts become.

Are you both operating on the same plane? It is possible that you are each approaching the problem from divergent views and your opinions are not even in the same ball park. You can recognize this when the two of you cannot sit together for a moment before contention sets in, in one form or another, but always prompted by the sensitivity of unresolved issues untouched by either of you. There is a remedy to begin treatment for this, it is called listening. The most important thing about listening is that you are not talking when you are listening, and in this case you are going to listen for a long time. It is important though, that you acknowledge what is being said, and that you elect not to respond to it at this time. Be sure to set a time for you to respond to the concerns raised by your partner, and that they know you intend to respond.

Elements of communication 101; listen, consider, and then speak words to edify. Respond with a soft answer, gentleness, and kindness. See (Proverbs 15:1, 17–18).

How much are you taking from the relationship without putting back?

> Let him that stole steal no more, rather let him labor that he may have to give to him that needeth. (Ephesians 4:28)

Stop taking from the relationship and start putting something back. If your partner is the one in need, then work to provide your partner with the rudimentary help to build him or her up in the relationship.

Have you become more apart from each other than a part of each other? Have you diminished your time together, put distance between each other, introduced other obligations that consume your time, or have you allowed for waning circumstances to rule over you?

If there is willingness, you can change these aspects of your circumstances. Give up something of lesser value so that you spend more time in the relationship, or sacrifice something of great value and commit in full to rebuilding your relationship.

Always in Remembrance (2 Peter 1:15)

1. Ever increasing harsh treatment is a symptom of _____ in the relationship.

2. Can you identify if your relationship has entered into a _____ cycle?

3. A relationship is reprobate when one or more persons are _____ to compromise.

4. Basic elements to communication include _____, considering what is said, and speaking words to edify.

5. A soft answer, gentleness, and kindness help to _____ tension in a relationship.

6. An _____ relationship is comprised of outbursts and outrageous behavior.

7. An intellectual relationship is too _____; little is communicated with THIS.

8. Your partner may be in need of being _____ in the relationship.

9. Closeness and time spent _____ helps to build up the relationship.

10. To succeed, you may be called upon to make _____ in your relationship.

Scripture Reference:
Titus 1:15–16; Proverbs 15:1, 17–18; Ephesians 4:28

VI. Building Success into the Relationship

Higher Ground Principle # 7

Build a virtuous cycle in your relationship through hard work.

In order to successfully build up a relationship, you must take the initiative to begin a virtuous cycle. Virtuosity does not come easily when a relationship has been in a state of decay for some time. It requires hard work, sacrifice, and the setting aside of your pride.

Begin the change by doing something positive. Build patterns of successes into your routines that encourage one another and that inspire kindness, gentleness, and favorable treatment. Remember the 5 Ss. This is a good time and place to start applying them aggressively.

Compliment, don't criticize

We are each gifted with an innate ability to identify others' weaknesses and short comings. We are never short of answers or suggestions to correct someone, no matter how insensitive or callous our suggestions may be. It is healthier to find some way to compliment your partner than to criticize him or her. It is painstakingly difficult to compliment someone when they have injured you, but it is doable and essential to repair a broken relationship. Adopt a system of behavior that enables you to be the kindest when you hurt the most.

Being kind to your partner when he has gorged the goodness out of you is how you become Christ like.

> And not only so, but we glory in tribulations also: knowing that tribulation worketh patience; And patience, experience; and experience, hope: And hope maketh not ashamed; because the love of God is shed abroad in our hearts by the Holy Ghost which is given unto us. (Romans 5:3–5)

Build consistency in your relationship

What is the most difficult task that you can be called upon to do in order to achieve success? The hardest work is to bring about change in your own mind when you are engaged in difficult circumstances and the life experiences you have to draw from are the same ones leading you to do the opposite of what's in your best interest. Your life's experiences have a tendency to push you to do the contrary of what you should do to repair the relationship. You must bring about a change in your state of mind, which encourages a new and different level of thinking. You must get your mind to the point that it will allow you to take the first step in a positive direction. Then, you can continue to take bigger and more frequent steps until you are running at the full speed of your mind in the direction of your loved one. You are to aspire to obtain peace. Be a blessing to your partner and don't allow yourself to be drawn in to the same level of his or her momentary state of mind. Don't recompense evil with evil, but rather, be the one with the renewed mind reminding yourself that this person is a very valuable part of your life. (Romans 12:14–18).

Here are valuable points to help you reconcile.

How much are you willing to risk to make a relationship work? We take risks going into business, changing jobs, moving, and driving to the corner store. Why are we so guarded with our emotions when it comes to our relationships? The answer simply lies in that we value other things in life based on their quantitative worth, but our relationships are valued solely on emotions. As we become less emotionally guarded, the intensity of our emotional reactions will decrease and our relationships will improve.

We must learn and put into practice ways to nourish the relationship. In marriage, as well as in other relationships, it might begin with more intimacy in sharing daily life experiences, exercising THIS one hundred percent of the time, setting aside time to be together, participating with each other, and alternating the things that are special to either one. Other ideas include dating and giving each other special little gifts. (Everyone likes pleasant surprises; be original with yours.)

Is there consensus of leadership, and acknowledgement to keep the relationship on track?

Two cannot make a democracy. One has to lead and make essential decisions, and the other should be willing to concede and consciously submit in agreement. Compromise is not the best solution in a relationship. A compromise between two persons may produce an undesirable result with lasting consequences and harboring of ill feelings. Submission, although strange to our ears, is the call of the Christian in a godly relationship. By making a conscious decision to concede, one also makes commitment to fully support the decision (1 Corinthians 11:3 and Ephesians 5:23).

How are decisions made in your relationship?

What method do you employ in your relationship for identifying problems and their causes? What is your plan for dealing with these issues and finding a way to repair them? Your response may be a shrug, or if you honestly want to resolve them, you might say, "I don't know".

Getting started does not have to be brutally painful, or extremely embarrassing, if it is born out of love. 1 Peter 4:8 reminds us that love shall cover a multitude of sins. The human mind has a propensity to stay focused on the negative. On occasion, I have delivered what I thought was great news only to have my joy dampened by a negative acknowledgement. You are familiar with these. They are the "prophets of doom" comments that we receive from family and friends. You tell your spouse, "Honey, we just paid off the Visa card," and her response is "Well, what are we going to do about the MasterCard?" It's sort of depressing, isn't it? I have found myself doing it. Instead of rejoicing at the good news, we cast gloom and cause guilt to arise in our relationship. We tend to cause guilt in each other when we should be the authors of joy for the people in our lives.

If you pause to think about how much you love and admire this person, perhaps your reaction would be one of support and encouragement. To begin this upward spiral, you must commit to inviting the Lord into your relationship. Identify the problem to focus on, and commit with your partner to pray for it together on a daily basis. Organize your thinking and plan to pray without bringing up what you think caused the problem (his laziness, her shopping, etc.), but pray only that the Lord will tenderize both your hearts and open your understanding that you may receive His guidance and know how to apply it. Your relationship will show improvement quickly.

What additional (new) value can you add to the relationship so that it does prosper?

This question should not be taken lightly. You need to ask yourself, "What proactive measures can I take to be encouraging to my partner?" This is an important fundamental for leading one another into caring and openness about the decisions that are to be made. One way to add value to the relationship is by not allowing life to become so routine that one or both of you lose heart and by letting the relationship become perfunctory without meaning. You do or say vain, hollow and empty things with little or no intent of executing them as part of a joint plan with accountability. You want to discuss plans with real timetables, budgets, and distribution of labor, as well as responsibility, and above all with real intent to fulfill them. This is it. This is how decisions get made in your relationship: with full participation from all participants.

Always in Remembrance (2 Peter 1:15)

1. By taking the initiative, you can start a _____ cycle.

2. Doing _____ things builds patterns of success.

3. The hardest work takes place in the _____.

4. Letting go of your _____ depends on how big of a risk you are willing to take.

5. Pleasant surprises _____ the relationship.

6. How _____ are made affect the overall health of the relationship.

7. How do you plan to resolve issues and _____ the relationship?

8. Nourishing the needs of your partner adds _____ and builds up the relationship.

Scripture Reference:
Romans 5:3–5; Romans 12:14–21; 1 Corinthians 11:3; Ephesians 5:22; 1 Peter 4:8

VII. Applying Word Knowledge

Higher Ground Principle # 8

Assert your right to leadership through sacrifice and service.

Are you Lording it over?

And why call ye me, Lord, Lord, and do not the
things which I say? (Luke 6:46)

In Christ's teachings, we have the basic rudiments prescribed for a healthy relationship. We are denying Him when we choose to do the contrary of what He desires that we do. If we are not obeying Him, then He is not our Lord.

Be worthy to call Him Lord.

It is inherent in our human nature to have others wait on us. That is why the travel and leisure industry is so prosperous. People like having someone to serve them, pick up after them, and feed them on time. Aside from the pandering of alcoholic beverages, being waited on and served is the trademark of Carnival Cruise Lines. These services and the form of treatment you get on a cruise are because you pay for it. It is something you buy. Being waited on is not something you buy in a personal relationship. It most certainly rubs contrary to any godly relationship between friends and family. The Christian attitude of service is all about something you give or do and not centered on material things and benefits that you get.

> He riseth from supper, and laid aside his garments; and took a towel, and girded himself. After that he poureth water into a bason, and began to wash the disciples' feet, and to wipe them with the towel wherewith he was girded. (John 13:4–5)

A true leader sets the example. He or she is willing to make sacrifices for the benefit of others. The leader in the family should constantly be on the lookout for opportunities that may arise where he or she can be of service to other family members. Likewise, every leader should be alert to opportunities to give up comfort as a sacrifice for someone else. In this fashion, the Word of God comes to light in that the one who serves the most is the greatest. Don't let your partner out-serve you.

> So after he had washed their feet, and had taken his garments, and was set down again, he said unto them, Know ye what I have done to you? Ye call me Master and Lord: and ye say well; for so I am. If I then, your Lord and Master, have washed your feet; ye also ought to wash one another's feet. For I have given you an example, that ye should do as I have done to you. Verily, verily, I say unto you, The servant is not greater than his lord; neither he that is sent greater than he that sent him. If ye know these things, happy are ye if ye do them. (John 13:12–17)

If you want joy and happiness in your present life, you must be willing to sacrifice your pride, your comfort, and your desire to be waited on in exchange for satisfying the needs and desires of your partner. You have this "god given" opportunity to be the leader in your relationship by demonstrating these Christ-like qualities of giving and serving first, without requiring recompense. Christ demonstrated this Himself by doing the lowliest of tasks for His disciples and did not ask anything of them for Himself. He told His disciples that He had given them an example so that they would do for others as He did for them. They witnessed unfathomable love and unyielding commitment on His part to serve them. Christ is not only our example, He is also our Lord, and the Lord is the one whom you must obey.

Always in Remembrance (2 Peter 1:15)

1.   *Exerting pressure on others to get what you want is* _____ *it over them.*

2.   *You deny Jesus's Lordship when you do differently than He* ___.

3.   *Expecting others to* _____ *us does not strengthen our relationships.*

4.   *The Christian attitude of service is defined in that one desires to* _____ .

5.   _____ *your preferences is a quality for Christian living.*

6.   *The* _____ *example of acceptable leadership is set by Jesus.*

7.   *The* _____ *of the family should be prepared to be of service to the others.*

8.   *A willingness to sacrifice will bring* _____ *and happiness to your life.*

Scripture Reference:
Luke 6:46; John 13:4–5; John 13:12–17

VIII. Qualities for Christian Living

Higher Ground Principle # 9

Live and walk by the higher and greater standard worthy of the Christian name.

As Christians, we have a very special charge and responsibility. We accepted Jesus Christ as our Lord to live according to the principles and precepts that He taught and that have been committed to us in God's Word. That responsibility carries us a bit further than just living it. It includes teaching biblical precepts to others. If you desire to have a godly relationship, no one is in greater need of knowing God's principles as you know them than the other person in your relationship.

However, before you can teach biblical precepts to others, you must have acquired knowledge from the Word of God for yourself. Then, when you know something, after you have put it into practice for yourself, you can offer it up and be the example. Being a Christian is a very high calling. You may have previously heard the term "high calling." It is not only a calling from above, but it is also a calling for you to rise higher or at least to rise above others. If your public or private behavior is the same as everybody else's, if you are reacting adversely to someone because you think it's cool or because that's the way people around you do it, or if you tell someone off because it's the popular thing to do, then you are no better than others in the world. In fact, you are being of the world and your conversation is in the world (Romans 1:32). Why would anyone—seeing the type of your behavior as not different than their own and their tormentors—want to follow you into the Kingdom of God? (2 Thessalonians 3:7).

You must move beyond the popular ways. You have to get past the worlds way of thinking and the lifestyle of the ungodly. Using the same thinking pattern as those around you will lead you into incongruous behavior untypical of a Christian. You need to realize that the Lord has made you better than what the world calls you out to be. You need to rise up with the Lord to a higher calling. This is what I want you to draw from God's Word in this series of teachings. It is up to you to take the initiative to make every one of your relationships work. Make your relationships with others who are important components to your life work. If you can't see yourself sharing a relationship with a particular person who is integral to your family unit and circle of friends or beneficial to your life, then you have a lot of work to do. First, gird up yourself. Then when you are better prepared, you can help to shore up the breaches in the other person's life (Galatians 6:2).

Most of the values that you have adopted into a relationship are not the values the Lord asks of you. In other words, your values might be, "I'm not going to put up with that because I am this and I am that," or "Because of my position in life," or "I'm older, therefore everybody has to respect me." That is not biblically correct. It is you that has to respect everyone. The Lord says the one who serves the most is going to be the greatest of all. Do you want to be great? Then you have to serve the needs of others regardless of their station in life, and you must get started today (Galatians 5:13).

As a Christian, bear in mind the qualities that permit you to live in the world peaceably with as little friction as possible in your relationships with others. This can be studied from two separate points of view. One view concerns yourself, and it is required that you not offend or cause abrasion to others (Philippians 1:10). We want to study that separately from the second view, which is what happens when someone offends you. What do you do then? I'm assuming you are not sure what the best course of action to take is, so I will share the Word's principles on this with you.

You need to adopt a code of conduct for handling offenses and abrasions, both when you are the cause and when others precipitate the cause. When others offend you, you have to have the right code of conduct in order for you to handle it correctly. Correctly means according to principles from the Word. An incorrect response may be considered popular in the eyes of others, but it is unbecoming behavior that makes you feel good at the expense of the other person and is contrary or inconsistent with the Word.

Your personal code of conduct is to not offend or cause abrasion to others.

Adopt a code of conduct for handling offenses and abrasions caused by others.

Always in Remembrance (2 Peter 1:15)

1. *Christians have a very special charge and* _____.

2. _____ *Jesus Christ as Lord in your life commits you to obeying Him.*

3. *Christians should know and* _____ *biblical principles to others.*

4. *Being a Christian is a very high* _____.

5. *Your* _____ *should not be the same as others.*

6. *You must apply the* _____ *taught by the Lord in your relationship.*

7. *You should have a* _____ *of conduct to apply in adverse situations.*

8. *Your personal code of conduct is not to* _____ *others.*

Scripture Reference:
Romans1:32; 2 Thessalonians 3:7; Galatians 6:2; Galatians 5:13;
1 Corinthians 13:11–12

IX. Offenses Committed by You

Your commitment as a card-carrying Christian is to be the peacemaker, the light bearer, and the salt of the earth to flavor life all around you. Before you step out to put these callings to work, you must ponder these precepts and fully embrace them with a commitment to carry them out. These precepts are means that minimize unnecessary pressure on you and on those in your proximity; the unnecessary pressures are caused by offenses you inflict and offenses inflicted upon you.

> And the seed whose fruit is righteousness is sown in peace by those who make peace. (James 3:18)

The Peacemaker

Higher Ground Principle # 10

Be a peacemaker who brings calm to your relationship.

Scripture Reference:

> Deceit is in the heart of them that imagine evil: but to the counsellor of peace is joy. (Proverbs 12:20)

Those who make peace do not accomplish it solely by their good deeds. We know from the history of wars that men do not appropriate enduring peace. When peace is brought on in a godly way, it is the product of a seed that bears righteousness as its fruit. That is to say, the means employed in the ensuing peace were means congruent with God's way and were right with God. A peacemaker, we may conclude, is a believer who is walking with God step for step in the footsteps of Jesus.

In the section of scripture we refer to as the Beatitudes, the Lord proclaims that peacemakers are blessed and that they shall be called the children of God (Matthew 5:9). This sets for us the light in which God has framed the value of a peacemaker. As the peacemaker, you become invaluable to the perseverance of the Church, and you become the preserver of peace in your relationships. If you desire to have a healthy relationship, you will need to cover it with peace and use peace as the safety net when things start to slip in your relationship. Only you can operate peace in your life, and you alone have been equipped by the Holy Ghost to do so in every relationship.

A peacemaker is best characterized as one who brings calm to a tumultuous situation. We saw previously a wonderful example of how this calm is manifested in Matthew 8:23–27 where the Lord enters a boat with the disciples, and is asleep while they battle a storm. The boat is about to sink and the disciples panic. They fear that they will sink and drown. (Having been in a severe storm in a small boat, I'm sympathetic to what was going on in the disciples' minds. One loses hope rather quickly, and a dreadful fear for life sets in fast.) The disciples finally, run to Jesus and say, "Save us Lord. We are perishing!" I'm reasonably sure that there were big exclamation marks at the end of that phrase. The Lord asks, "Why are you afraid?" in a calm voice. Then He rebukes the winds and the sea, and it becomes perfectly calm. His affect on others was to bring calm and, as peacemaker, to bring ensuing peace. This is what you are called upon to bring into your relationship.

As the peacemaker, you are equipped with various attributes that prepare you for the duty of improving relationships. There are other attributes essential to that role, and I encourage you to embrace two other precepts that, when applied, invoke the fullness of God's power over the prevailing circumstances. One of these concepts is to be the salt of the earth, and the other is to be the light of the world.

Always in Remembrance (2 Peter 1:15)

1. *Christians are called upon to be* _____.

2. *Applying biblical precepts will diminish unnecessary* _____
in your relationship.

3. _____ *peace is appropriated through godly works.*

4. *Peacemakers are* _____.

5. *Peacemakers shall be called the* _____ *of God.*

6. *As peacemaker, you become the* _____ *of peace
in your relationship.*

7. *You are* _____ *to operate peace in your
relationship.*

8. *A peacemaker brings* _____ *into a tumultuous
situation.*

9. *A peacemaker's* _____ *on others is to calm
them*

Scripture Reference:
James 3:18; Proverbs 12:20; Matthew 5:9; Matthew 8:23-27

The Salt of the Earth

Higher Ground Principle # 11

Keep the salt flavor for God's Word in you from diluting by temptation and sin.

Ye are the salt of the earth: but if the salt have lost his *savour,* wherewith shall it be salted? ...

Lord Jesus's exhortation to you is that you compare your usefulness to that of salt. If you are the salt of the earth, you are the one who infuses flavor into the earth, at least in a spiritual sense. If you have lost your saltiness, then who is going to flavor you? Where is your flavor going to come from? This is the comparison the Lord is making. You are the salt. You are the one God has called through Jesus. You are the one that has been given the charge. You are the one that has been given the responsibility. If you ignore or refuse to apply these principles in your life, where is your help going to come from? You will be salt less! What good are you then?

... It is thenceforth good for nothing ...

When you act like everyone else around you is acting, you are good for nothing, because you have lost your salt. You have lost your high calling for what you have been called to be. What good are you then?

... but to be cast out, and to be trodden under foot of men ... (Matthew 5:13–14)

Our joint commitment with the Lord is to be peacemakers, to be light bearers, and to be the salt of the earth to flavor the lives of others around us. When you are at peace, the people around you receive that peace, and they will also become peaceful. When you are vociferous, noisy, and argumentative, that is exactly what you will give off, and everybody around you will be inclined to treat each other, and especially you, the same way. But remember, you are the salt; it is you who adds the flavor. Therefore, you cannot expect others to be the peacemakers who calm the situation since they simply don't know how. They lack the wherewithal to add godly flavor. It is incumbent upon you to be the initiator and to apply these precepts. You have to do it. You alone have the salt in you to flavor the situation.

If you are the salt, then you cannot afford to lose your flavor. If you lose your flavor, what or who is going to flavor you? When salt loses its flavor, it is good for nothing. It can't be used. Salt is not only used for seasoning, it is also used as a preservative in food.

Bacalao is salted codfish, which can last forever without refrigeration. Likewise, the salt of God's Word preserves us. When we are preserved in the salt, we can go anywhere. It doesn't matter who you come in contact with. You are still going to maintain your saltiness because that's what you have in you. It's a good analogy in terms of the Word of God. When you have the Word of God deep in your heart with conviction—when you are not allowing anyone to come along and rinse it out of your life with a bad word or with a bad attitude—you are fulfilling the high calling. When someone has a bad attitude, you're going to turn to him and say, "Gee, are you having a rough day? Perhaps I can pray for you." Or you might say something very nice to that person and they are going to back off, because in Proverbs 15:1 the Bible says, "A gentle answer turns away wrath" (NASB). But if someone is having a hard time, or making a hard time of something, and you step out and give them an equally hard time, then the situation is only going to get worse for everyone. Without its flavor, salt is completely useless.

> Salt is good: but if the salt have lost his saltness, wherewith will ye season it? Have salt in yourselves, and have peace one with another. (Mark 9:50)

When you live the precept of salt, you are going to have peace. God's Word exhorts you to have peace and to be the peacemaker with those that are around you.

> Salt is good: but if the salt have lost his savour, wherewith shall it be seasoned? It is neither fit for the land, nor yet for the dunghill; but men cast it out. He that hath ears to hear, let him hear. (Luke 14:34–35)

Salt is a mineral; it has chlorine and sodium. When these two elements are together, they serve a purpose. You can use these combined elements to accomplish wonderful things. But when it has lost the flavor, all you have is a block of white powder that is good for nothing. It won't even decompose. That describes you when you are walking according to the sin of the world instead of walking by the Word of God. You are not going to influence change in anyone's life with your negative attitude or by retorting with a smart saying when what the person really needs is a blessing in the form of kindness or compassion.

Always in Remembrance (2 Peter 1:15)

1.   *As Christians, we are committed to be* _____.

2.   *We are commanded to be the* _____ *of the earth.*

3.   *If you are the salt, where does your* _____ *come from?*

4.   *If salt loses its flavor, it is* _____ *for nothing.*

5.   *We flavor and preserve others'* _____ *with God's Word.*

6.   *By being at peace, we* _____ *of our peace with others around us.*

The Light of the World

Higher Ground Principle # 12

Illuminate darkened hearts, help bear another's heavy load, and bring cheer to the sad.

> Ye are the light of the world. [Called to be a light of the world; this is another really good thing.] A city that is set on a hill cannot be hid. (Matthew 5:14)

As a bearer of light, you are committed to bring light into dark situations and dark places. You are the center of hope, goodness, kindness, and godliness. (How many of you would like to join the club, the Light Bearers?) Light Bearers illuminate darkened hearts, bring cheer into the otherwise lackluster lives of people around them, help to bear the load weighing others down, and remove obstacles that obscure the vision from before their brethren's eyes. If you want, you too can join in this purpose, which is led by Jesus Christ.

> Matthew 5:16
> Let your light so shine before men that they may see your good works, [that they might see the goodness, that they might see that you are at the center of hope, that they can see the Godliness in you], and glorify your Father which is in heaven.

The concept I want you to think of here is that you are a beacon of light in a world of darkness. You bring light into the dark situations and the dark places around you. You are this beacon of light that can only be extinguished by you. Yes, you can dim your light if you put a cover over yourself and hide that glorious light, but that light should be burning furiously within you. The light in you should be burning so bright that you have to let it out or explode. You have to let that shining light permeate forth into the pervasive darkness of the world.

If you were standing in a dark room and lit a match, the little bit of light from that match would dispel the darkness. One little ray of light dispels darkness, and that's you! Wherever you are, and however dark the situation may be, you are the light, and it is incumbent upon you to bear that light. From now on you're going to let that light shine. You're going to polish the outside and the inside of the lens to make sure that God's light gets reflected through.

In 2005, my twelve-year-old daughter, Dolores, and I made the 203-step climb up a narrow spiraling, scary staircase to the top of the tallest lighthouse in Florida, the Ponce De Leon Inlet Lighthouse. The most impressive thing I learned that day is that the climb was made daily to polish the inside and the outside of the lens and to turn the light on so that ships could see it at night and in dense fog. The keepers did everything to increase its illumination in order to save human lives and precious cargo.

Likewise, we are charged every day with the responsibility to climb the wonderful, blessed, and safe steps to the Lord and polish our lenses. When we come to the Lord, we are renewed in mind and in spirit. We are revitalized and made able to preserve precious lives and keep valuable human cargo secure. You are going to increase your lumens, because you are going to put more and more of the Word of God into your life. You are going to live more and more by the Word of God. You're going to study Matthew, Chapters 5–7, the Sermon on the Mount and learn it thoroughly, because it is one of the best teachings on how to live a Christian life. I challenge you to read those chapters in the book of Matthew and to study and understand every word. This is what will increase the lumens in your spiritual life.

Always in Remembrance (2 Peter 1:15)

1. *Light bearers* _____ *darkened hearts.*

2. *Light bearers must polish their lenses* _____ *by studying the Word of God.*

3. *Your light can* _____ *others to salvation and peaceful lives.*

4. *The* _____ *in you can be dimmed or extinguished only if you allow it to be.*

5. *A light is not lit to be* _____*from view.*

6. *You have been illuminated by the light of* _____.

Scripture Reference:
Matthew 5:13-14; Proverbs 15:1; Mark 9:50; Luke 14:34-35

Ten Points of Light

Higher Ground Principle # 13

Let God's light into your heart by relating positively with others.

The Ten Commandments teach us how to have and maintain a relationship with God. The Sermon on the Mount teaches us how to righteously live the doctrine of a Christian life. Now we can learn from the Apostle Peter how to live rightly with men. I've termed this the Ten Points of Light. When applied, these ten principles will shed the great light of understanding into your heart.

Here are the biblical keys for how to get it done, how to overcome the propensity to offend others, and how to minimize or avoid being offended by others. There are ten points of light in the following passage that gives instruction on how to live godly lives among men.

> Having your *conversation honest* among the Gentiles: that, whereas they speak against you as evildoers, they may by your *good works*, which they shall behold, glorify God in the day of visitation. *Submit yourselves to every ordinance of man* for the Lord's sake: whether it be to the king, as supreme; Or unto governors, as unto them that are sent by him for the punishment of evildoers, and for the praise of them that do well. For so is the will of God, that *with well doing ye may put to silence the ignorance of foolish men:* As free, and *not using your liberty for a cloke of maliciousness,* but as the servants of God. *Honour all* men. *Love the brotherhood. Fear God. Honour the king.* 1 Peter 2:12–17

Be honest (in everything)
If someone comes up with a grand scheme that sounds good because you are going to profit from it, but it is not honest, then it is incumbent upon you to walk away from it. Prosperity derived

from unscrupulous means may appear to be fantastic at the time, but soon it will work against you and cause ruin to take root in your life (Proverbs 1:10). Be honest in everything. Just ask yourself, "What would Jesus do?" Would He do this? You are obligated to act as Jesus would because you are His representative. Those of you that understand law can appreciate that if you are His agent, you have an agency relationship with Jesus Christ. The things that you commit to here on earth are binding Him who is in Heaven (Matthew 16:19). As agents of Jesus Christ, we don't want to give the wrong impression. We always want to give the right impression. Being honest is critical to having good relationships with everyone around you.

Do good works (in every way)

Don't just say, "I'm going to do this because it is good for this person, but I'm not going to do it for that person." Do good in every way for everyone. There are no exceptions when it comes to doing good. It's a way of life. The following is what is required of you: changing your way of life so that you live a godly lifestyle and letting those lumens of light shine through brighter and brighter. You become saltier and saltier, and you have more and more flavor to season events around you. When somebody licks you, they'll say, "Mmm, this tastes good." (I mean this as a figure of speech, not literally).

Obey all laws and regulations (do not take shortcuts that violate ordinances)

Do not take shortcuts if they're in violation of ordinances. When you get to a stop sign, it means stop. That is an ordinance. It does not mean slow down, and if nobody is coming, roll through it. If you get into the practice of doing that—doing less than what is required—one day you're going to do it at the wrong time and in the wrong place. Then it will either be an incrimination to you or to them who you witness to. They are going to say, "Oh, and that's a Christian, hmm!" Don't tell me that you haven't had that experience. You know that any of us Bible-carrying Christians are easily identified, but what about when we are not carrying our Bibles?

This is the opposite of the effect we want to have on others. We are to be blameless and harmless, without fault and shine as lights in the world. (Philippians 2:15) The world should know who we are at all times by our behavior and our obedience to laws, ordinances, and regulations. You cannot just ignore them and expect to be regarded as a disciple of Christ.

Always do the right thing (even if it's not to your favor)

You are going to be tremendously challenged to always do the right thing, even when it does not appear to be in your favor. We are constantly facing situations where we might feel that we can get away without having to do the right thing, just this one time. You have to do the right thing every time! You can't allow yourself to lavish in this weakness. You have to think of the life you live as if it were the thickness of your armor, and every time that you deviate from this Christian requirement you put a kink in your armor. You know what armor does: armor protects from oncoming arrows. They go "bing" on impact, and they bounce off. If the armor takes a blow from a sword, it dents the armor and most likely prevents injury. That's how armor protects, and you've got this armor of God around you. But every time that you deviate from the Christian walk by not doing the Christian thing, you are saying, "Well, I know this is the right thing to do, but I'm not going to do it today because it is probably not a sin if I don't do it. If I don't do what I know to be the right thing, I have not sinned". Well that's not true. What the Word says is that if you know it is the right thing to do and you refuse to do it, it is sin: "Therefore to him that knoweth to do good, and doeth it not, to him it is sin" (James 4:17). When you fail to do the right thing, you abandon the protection of God's shield and become vulnerable to the fiery darts of the adversary and the crippling blows of life.

Don't use Christianity to beat others down (avoid putting guilt trips on others)

Resist the temptation to use Christianity to beat others down. Employ every bit of mental energy for self control to avoid putting guilt trips on others. We do this to each other. We do this amongst ourselves from friend to friend, and we do this to our family. We often violate the trust our closest friends put in us, and cause our relationships to break down. You may sarcastically say to someone, "Well, that's a good Christian way to behave!" That is not a blessing. What would be a blessing is to teach the person the scripture and to help them comprehend the godly principle involved. It is usually someone very close to you that you beat down with the Word. That's the meaning of the phrase, "Not using your liberty for a cloak of maliciousness." You're using the cloak of Christianity, "Well, I'm holier than thou," to beat someone down. That's not the right way to teach Christian principles to others. The way to teach is to demonstrate biblical principles by your application of them, not by making people feel bad or by making them feel inferior. All that is accomplished when you make them feel bad is to turn the other person off. If you thought you were witnessing to your brother, sister, mother, father, or spouse and you beat them down with the Word; your salt has lost its flavor for that person. If you've ever been beaten down with the Word, you know exactly what I'm talking about. If you've ever beaten someone down with the Word, you know that you need to stop doing that. You need to just not do that anymore. .

Be first a servant of God (Put God first in everything you do)

If you find yourself in a situation where you are unsure of what to do, ask yourself, if Jesus Christ were in this position, what would Jesus do? Then do as He would do. If you're not sure, ask Him, because you've got His spirit. The Holy Spirit will communicate and tell you and put the right conviction in your heart. Being first a servant to God requires that you emulate Jesus. He is the only example to follow. As a servant to God, you must know what things God requires of you in any given situation or circumstance. The conclusion is that you will do what God wants first and foremost, regardless of how much it might conflict with someone else's or your own desire. "What does God want me to do?" is always a good question to ask. If you are not sure, say "Gee, what would Jesus do in this situation?" Read the book of Matthew, Chapters 5 through 7, and study the Sermon on the Mount. You will see that it covers every principle for putting God first.

Don't dishonor or disrespect others (put off your airs of superiority)

The best way for you not to dishonor or disrespect others is to learn and practice honoring and respecting behavior. Disrespect and dishonor of others occurs when you put on airs of superiority or when you, by what you say, make others feel that they are inferior both intentionally and unintentionally. Never allow yourself to utter something that could make another person feel small or to make others look small. That dishonors and disrespects others. Everyone knows who you are. For example, if you're the boss, everybody knows. If they don't know, it's not going to be very long before they know. So you don't need to walk in and say, "Hello, everybody. I'm the boss." They already know. What you're saying to them is, "You idiots, don't you know that I'm the boss, and those of you that don't know I'm the boss are a bunch of idiots. I'm telling you that I'm the boss, so now you know, you bunch of idiots." We do the same in many aspects of our lives. If you're the parent, your child knows that you're the parent. You don't have to beat them over the head about it. Whoever you are in your position in life, everyone who needs to know who you are knows who you are. You don't need to lord your title over them. Just be your normal self. Be yourself, and people will respect you. Show respect to others, and earn their respect.

Express love to those in the church family (not just on Sundays when we see each other)

Express love to those in the Church family, not only when you get together on Sunday but throughout the week, day-by-day. Every moment presents a new opportunity for you to demonstrate your love. It is up to you to create the opportunity to show your love to someone else. You can show your love to others by staying in contact and by lending your help when it is needed. Say, for example, a brother is ill and needs help with food shopping or picking up a prescription. You would not necessarily know this unless you were involved. You wouldn't be helpful unless you knew that this particular help was needed. I know we all love each other, and that's wonderful. I know that if there is anything that any one of us can do

69

for another, we would not hesitate to do it. I know that you know that too. But you need to express ongoing love. You can express ongoing love by being in contact with each other on a regular basis, if only just to say hello, to see what you could pray for, or to see how you can be a blessing to that brother or sister. There's nothing wrong with making a "love call" or "love visit." Today, we have text messaging and cell phones, we have house phones, we have e-mail, we have Blackberries, and we have the U.S. Postal Service for staying in touch. We can communicate if we so desire. There's nothing to stop us from communicating with one another. If you're not communicating with one another, it means that during the entire week you're not giving yourself the opportunity to bless a brother or sister or to be blessed by a brother or sister. You need to change that way of living. It's one of the keys to living a life full of light to be able to be a blessing, give a blessing, and receive a blessing. Express love to those in the Church family.

Hold God and the things of God in reverential fear (don't compromise your godliness)

Reverential fear is a good term to know, because it is not this shaky kind of fear we associate with horror movies or spooky houses. It is a fear that comes from knowing that God is omnipotent, and that if He wanted to, He could put an end to all this, right here, right now. We cannot do a thing to stop Him. We cannot change the will of God (Numbers 16:31–33). What God has put into motion will stay in motion until He stops it. Not one of us can change that. You have to express reverential fear of God. Your heart should cry out with intensity, "God, I want to do your will. God, I want to respect your things, the things that you've asked of me. I want to obey you because You are God and I am Your servant as well as Your child. But I am first in a relationship of being a servant to do Your will, and then I'm in a relationship as Your child." Our choice is obvious, though limited. We have free will, and we can choose not to do it, but not to do His will is not a good choice (Luke 12:5).

Honor the elected or appointed heads of state (although you may not agree with them)

Sometimes you look at the people who are running the government and say, "Where did they come from?" You may think that you could do a better job, but you are not the one who was elected. You are not the one who was appointed. But you have a responsibility, if you want to live a peaceful life, to bring honor to the heads of state. Not because they deserve it, not because they earned it, and not because you're in agreement with them, but because God tells you that if you are to live a peaceful life, this is what you must do. Honor the elected and appointed heads of state. Just as God works with you and through you to accomplish His purpose, God may just as well be working to accomplish His will through those officials you are so disappointed in. You don't know what God is up to with respect to how He uses anyone. For the most part, we are not sure of exactly how He is using us. We should pray for our officials, and we should honor them, as well.

The ten precepts described above are like ten points of light. Obey these ten rules in order to live a peaceful life and to shed light into the darkness of the world. If not, you are not the solution but part of the problem. You don't want to be found in that position. John 15:8 reads, "Herein is my Father glorified, that you bear much fruit." God is glorified when you bear fruit. "So shall you be my disciples." Not only is God glorified when you bear fruit in your life, but that fruit is how you are identified as a disciple of Jesus Christ.

So what does it mean to bear fruit? To bear fruit in your life, in the context that is spoken of here, is to bring godliness into your life and into the life of others. It is really a simple precept to understand especially in light of Galatians 5:22–23, which spells out the fruit of the spirit. Are you bringing godliness into your life? Are you bringing godliness into the situation that you are in at work, at home, or wherever you happen to be? If you are not, you are not glorifying God, if you are, you are glorifying God. You are bearing fruit, and your identity is that of a disciple of Jesus.

The scripture further tells us in John 8:9–11 that "As the Father has loved me, so have I loved you; continue ye in my love. If you keep my commandments, you shall abide in my love, even as I have kept my Father's commandments and abide in his love. These things have I spoken unto you, that my joy might remain in you, and *that* your joy may be full."

Are you full of joy? Yes? Good! If you are not, what is described above is among the principles you need to operate in your life so that you may be full of joy. If you are full of joy, you need to continue in those precepts to maintain a life filled with joy. God makes it so simple, doesn't He? Now that you have the correct and proper recipe, you can see that it is easy to do. You want to continue being the salt of the earth, because if you are not the salt, you are useless. If you lose your flavor, you are not good to anyone. You have to maintain your flavor. You have to be that shining bright light in the darkness of this world. If you cover that light, then you are just not living up to God's expectation of you. That's the way you should think about these callings so that God's expectation of you is fulfilled. That is why He has given you all these wonderful tools. He says, "Now that I have given you the tools to work with, this is what I expect you to do. Now go and live up to it". If you do as He has asked, you will notice things start to turn to the positive; conflict will dissipate out of your life. I'm not saying that everybody else is going to do the right thing for you. That should not be your expectation. What it assures is that you will be walking with the Holy Spirit. He shall not forsake you or allow your temptations to be above what you are able to handle. The expectation is that you do the correct things according to the high calling that God has called you to.

Always in Remembrance: *2 Peter 1:15*

1. *Be _____ in everything.*

2. *Do _____ works in every way.*

3. *_____ all laws and regulations.*

4. *Always work to meet God's _____.*

5. *Don't _____ Christianity to beat others down.*

6. *Be _____ a servant of God.*

7. *Don't dishonor or _____ others.*

8. *Express _____ to the family in the Church.*

9. *_____ God in reverential fear.*

10. *_____ the elected and appointed heads of state.*

Scripture Reference:
Matthew Chapters 5–7; 1 Peter 2:12–17; James 4:17; John 15:8;
John 8:9–11;

X. Handling Those Who Offend You

Higher Ground Principle # 14

Follow the example of forgiveness given by Jesus.

You thirst for instruction on right daily living. Meanwhile, the Bible's instruction stares you in the face. But you refuse to accept this instruction because it does not align with your own preconceived ideas of what is just, moral, or ethical. You prefer to apply the meaning of these precepts according to your understanding and how you want others to apply them to you. Each of us is tempted with the thought of being the exception to God's rules, especially if His rules do not conform to your lifestyle. Why do you think you're tempted to think this way? Where did you get the idea that you merit or have earned such a privilege from God?

The Bible tells us that we were saved (redeemed) when we were in our worst state—dead in trespasses and sin. We were condemned to death, but Jesus took our place at the execution and died in our place (Isaiah 53:5). If anything, we are debtors to Him for His substitution for us in what we refer to as Calvary.

No person should make reference to Calvary unless they have truly accepted Jesus as Lord and are doing His will by means of their own free will, choice, and obedience. (Matthew 7:21–23)

In effect, we are without excuse not to be 100 percent obedient to God. He sent His Son to teach us and show us God's will for man, and He purchased mankind back by sacrificing His life. Jesus gave His life in payment for all of man's wrong doing and paid the price so that mankind could return to God. Consider these two things He asks of you in return.

> But I say unto you, That whosoever is angry with his brother without a cause shall be in danger of the judgment: and whosoever shall say to his brother, Raca, shall be in danger of the council: but whosoever shall say, Thou fool, shall be in danger of hell fire. Therefore if thou bring thy gift to the altar, and there rememberest that thy brother hath ought against thee; Leave there thy gift before the altar, and go thy way; *first be reconciled to thy brother*, and then come and offer thy gift. *Agree with thine adversary quickly*, whiles thou art in the way with him; lest at any time the adversary deliver thee to the judge, and the judge deliver thee to the officer, and thou be cast into prison. Verily I say unto thee, Thou shalt by no means come out thence, till thou hast paid the uttermost farthing. (Matthew 5:22–26)

1. Be reconciled to your brother.

2. Agree with your adversary quickly.

These are two specific instructions directly from the Lord that teach you how to handle conflict with others. Do not assume that you are okay with God while you have an unresolved conflict with a brother in Christ. Your responsibility is to clean it up and come to God with a pure heart. Most of us don't enjoy being in a state of conflict with others, but some languish in it and refuse to overcome their pride. That prevents them from dealing with their error. This is a carnal state of the mind, and when the mind is unwilling to change, the Word says that the mind is reprobate (2 Corinthians 13:5–7). You are not instructed to go and straighten out other people. Rather, you are told to straighten out yourself for these two reasons:

1. So that your offerings are acceptable to God.

God prefers obedience over sacrifices. (1 Samuel 15:22) If you fail or refuse to change your mind concerning those with whom you have conflict, then you are disobedient to God's instruction. This example is prevalent for married men who dishonor their wives and cause their prayers to be hindered. 1 Peter 3:7

2. To avoid real big problems with secular authorities.

God is merciful and extends His mercy to the meek and humble. When you are prideful and decide to take matters into your own hands, you take God out of the picture and cast yourself into the hands of the rulers of the world. You become subject to their ungodly and unjust ways. By settling the matter quickly, you remain humble and in fellowship with God.

God's disposition on offenses to you or by you is best reflected in the following verses in Matthew 18. He will not tolerate your misbehavior, nor will He tolerate others' mistreatment of His little ones. God has appointed Angels to watch over His people, and they have instant access to God if they need to intervene for God's people.

> Woe unto the world because of offenses! For it must needs be that offenses come; but woe to that man by whom the offense cometh! Wherefore if thy hand or thy foot offend thee, cut them off, and cast them from thee: it is better for thee to enter into life halt or maimed, rather than having two hands or two feet to be cast into everlasting fire. And if thine eye offend thee, pluck it out, and cast it from thee: it is better for thee to enter into life with one eye, rather than having two eyes to be cast into hell fire. Take heed that ye *despise not one of these little ones*; for I say unto you, That in heaven their angels do always behold the face of my Father which is in heaven. (Matthew 18:7–10)

Always in Remembrance: *2 Peter 1:15*

1. You were _____ from sin and death while you were in your worst state.

2. You thirst for instruction on _____ daily living.

3. Before worshipping God, you should first be _____ with your partner.

4. You should _____ with an adversary quickly.

5. You are to _____ out yourself so that your offerings are acceptable to God.

6. You are to agree quickly with adversaries to _____ bigger issues with secular authorities.

Scripture Reference:
Matthew 5:22–26; 2 Corinthians 13:5–7; Matthew 18:7–10

XI. Handling Quarrels among Christians

Higher Ground Principle # 15

Avoid quarrels; do not trespass against others.

> Moreover if thy brother shall trespass against thee,
> go and tell him his fault between thee and him alone:
> if he shall hear thee, thou hast gained thy brother.
> (Matthew 18:15–17)

What does it mean for your brother or sister to trespass against you? A trespass is a major violation of exercising your will over another without regard for their rights or feelings. In a relationship, many opportunities arise daily to commit trespasses against each other. There are many types of trespasses, but we will examine only a few in order to increase our understanding of what is communicated in the Bible on this topic.

Here is what God's Word defines as trespasses we commit against each other:

1. Grieves your soul—makes you feel emotional illness.

2. Affronts you—causes painful confrontation and provokes an ill response.

3.   Abuses you—unfair bullying; someone who is more eloquent, talks louder, or uses an economic, emotional or personal advantage over you to get their way.

4.   Gossips and besmirches your standing among others in the Church—brings false accusations, tale-bearing, tattle-telling.

5.   Is injurious to your estate—puts you down.

One of the major exhortations from the Word is that you take the initiative to draw a person's attention to your feelings if he or she commits a trespass against you. Our tendency is to sulk and harbor ill feelings until the person voluntarily comes around and apologizes. We may try sending subtle messages by mistreating them or ignoring them until they come around. Worse yet, sometimes we send an envoy to carry our message of hurt to the person's close friends. These messengers are often ill-equipped and not delicate in their delivery. The end result is that a situation that might have been easily resolved gets escalated to a stage where friendships and relationships are put in jeopardy. Such an error should not be committed, since we know that the spiritual solution is for you to go and tell him his fault between you and him alone. If he hears your point of view and appreciates what has transpired, you will gain your partner's respect, and the relationship will be healed.

Nonetheless, if the other person has a lesser understanding of godly principles, you will have to exercise greater caution in your approach so that they do not perceive it as an unprovoked confrontation. In such cases, you must use a didactic approach to teach the biblical principle before you bring up the fault. Otherwise, the uninstructed person may be offended and pushed away erroneously, thinking that you are treating them unfairly.

> And through thy knowledge shall the weak brother perish, for whom Christ died? But when ye sin so against the brethren, and wound their weak conscience, ye sin against Christ. Wherefore, if meat make my brother to offend, I will eat no flesh while

the world standeth, lest I make my brother to offend.
(1 Corinthians 8:11–13)

Doing something to exploit another person's lesser understanding of God's Word or lesser ability regarding spiritual matters, or compelling another to sin through their weakness, is a sin. You must guard that you are not the source of such a provocation of another to sin. This issue is speaking to the one who commits the offense. The reminder is for you, the aggrieved, to abstain from doing things that would offend others and abstain from offending others in order to achieve your own vain and self-indulgent pleasure. If a partner or associate offends you, you need to go back and review Matthew 18 for instruction on how to overcome and get past any anger or desire for revenge.

> But why dost thou judge thy brother? or why dost thou set at nought thy brother? for we shall all stand before the judgment seat of Christ. For it is written, As I live, saith the Lord, every knee shall bow to me, and every tongue shall confess to God. So then every one of us shall give account of himself to God. Let us not therefore judge one another any more: but judge this rather, that no man put a stumblingblock or an occasion to fall in his brother's way. (Romans 14:10–13)

> And the King shall answer and say unto them, Verily I say unto you, Inasmuch as ye have done it unto one of the least of these my brethren, ye have done it unto me. (Matthew 25:40)

The Bible is very specific about God's view of men when it comes to offending one another. We are boldly reminded that all will stand before the Lord, at the judgment seat of Christ, to give account for our every action. There is no escape from this for anyone. You should take the initiative in your relationship not to be offensive or judgmental of others so that you are not held accountable on the

Day of Judgment. The Lord reminds us that offending even the least of these, His brethren, is the same as offending Him. The scriptures are replete in expressing this principle. Even the Law of Moses was not silent concerning matters between the brethren. The following passages are enlightening when considering God's point of view on handling conflict in our relationships.

> And the LORD spake unto Moses, saying, If a soul sin, and commit a trespass against the LORD, and lie unto his neighbour in that which was delivered him to keep, or in fellowship, or in a thing taken away by violence, or hath deceived his neighbour; Or have found that which was lost, and lieth concerning it, and sweareth falsely; in any of all these that a man doeth, sinning therein: Then it shall be, because he hath sinned, and is guilty, that he shall restore that which he took violently away, or the thing which he hath deceitfully gotten, or that which was delivered him to keep, or the lost thing which he found, Or all that about which he hath sworn falsely; he shall even restore it in the principal, and shall add the fifth part more thereto, and give it unto him to whom it appertaineth, in the day of his trespass offering. (Leviticus 6:1–5)

> Thou shalt not defraud thy neighbour, neither rob him: the wages of him that is hired shall not abide with thee all night until the morning. Thou shalt not curse the deaf, nor put a stumblingblock before the blind, but shalt fear thy God: I am the LORD. Ye shall do no unrighteousness in judgment: thou shalt not respect the person of the poor, nor honour the person of the mighty: but in righteousness shalt thou judge thy neighbour. Thou shalt not go up and down as a talebearer among thy people: neither shalt thou stand against the blood of thy neighbour: I am the LORD. Thou shalt not hate thy brother in thine

heart: thou shalt in any wise rebuke thy neighbour, and not suffer sin upon him. Thou shalt not avenge, nor bear any grudge against the children of thy people, but thou shalt love thy neighbour as thyself: I am the LORD. (Leviticus 19:13–18)

When that Christian brother (your sister, wife, husband, friend, child, parent, employer, employee, or someone else) does offend you, you are not to let your displeasure fester into a secret malicious plot to get even or weave a plan with which to bring him down. You should first make a substitution for him. Put yourself in his place—this is what Christ did for you. Think about what this person might be going through at the moment, and don't dwell so much on how hurt your feelings are. Have a compassionate attitude instead of an insulted attitude. Then, do as Matthew 18:15 instructs, Go and tell him his fault... We usually stop reading right here. There is no period after fault. We are not told to go and tell him off. We are told to discuss the matter privately with him.

Our relationships can improve substantially if we put more of Christ and less of ourselves into our thinking and handling of issues that arise. You may first want to take inventory of your own shortcomings. For example, consider how you respond to things and how you perceive others, any inbred attitudes from your childhood and upbringing that are different from your partner's. Remember that we are each made differently and uniquely. Couple that with your unique set of life experiences and how different they may have been for someone else. In fact, someone else in the same circumstance may not have perceived the experiences the same as you. Being patient and understanding instead of angry and insulted is the best approach to solving problems that arise in your relationship.

Always in Remembrance*: 2 Peter 1:15*

1. When someone offends you, it _____ your soul and makes you feel emotional illness.

2. An affront causes painful confrontation and _____ an ill response.

3. Abuse and unfair _____ occurs when someone uses their talents to take advantage of others.

4. Gossip is a root for false _____ of others.

5. Tale-bearing is _____ and puts the other person down.

6. Tattle-telling is very _____ to the victim.

Scripture Reference:
Matthew 18:15–17; 1 Corinthians 8:11–13; Romans 14:10–13; Matthew 25:40; Leviticus 6:1–5; Leviticus 19:13–18

Maintaining Good Relationships:

Higher Ground Principle # 16

Maintain peace, love, and joy in the Church and in your relationship.

In this section, we want to expound on preserving purity and holiness in the Church. The problem we face in the Church is that we are trying to maintain good relationships with each other by applying the standards of the world (Gr. *aion* = 'this age'), as the world defines a relationship. The world is not your friend; it's your enemy. Therefore, any behavior according to the world is contrary to your better good in the Church. In fact, anything in your life that is not of or from God works against you, even if you don't realize it at the time (Romans 12:2).

The Word calls us to maintain peace, love, and joy within the Church, against such there is no law. Regarding everyone else outside the Church, you simply want to come to the quickest and easiest resolution so that you don't get entangled with it. In the Church, you are charged to forgive and bring peace between you and your brethren.

You must be sure that your personal relationships are devoid of sarcasm, conflict, and abrasive behavior, as is common behavior in the world today. You can avoid these undesirable characteristics by changing your attitude, if it is a confronting attitude, and pursuing a gentler and kinder approach. Perhaps you put yourself in your partner's place or sacrifice your point of view until the crisis blows over. Outright accusations are discouraged, because they tend to raise angry and defensive responses.

Remember that the only thing you can control in a confrontation is yourself. You can keep from railing accusations and driving the conversation further into the negative. At some point in the discussion, it is more prudent to stay quiet and let the other person vent. Hopefully, their tirade will be short-lived, and there won't be any ranting that might spark a negative response from you. Keep your emotions in check at all times.

A gentle answer turns away wrath, but a harsh word stirs up anger. (Proverbs 15:1; NASB)

Always in Remembrance: *2 Peter 1:15*

1. No one likes a confronting _____.

2. It is best to let the other person _____ *down.*

3. Railing accusations cause others to become _____ *and either attack or clam up.*

4. Be in _____ *of your emotions when you approach a brother to resolve a matter.*

5. The only perfect one is _____.

6. A _____ *answer turns away wrathful anger.*

Scripture Reference:
Matthew 18:15–17; 1 Corinthians 8:11–13; Romans 14:10–13; Matthew 25:40; Leviticus 6:1–7; Leviticus 19:8–18; Romans 12:2

XII. The Witness of the Church

Higher Ground Principle #17

Be a winner in every situation.

How many of us would like to win every argument? Today, you are going to learn how God designed it for you never to lose an argument.

> But if he will not hear thee, then take with thee one or two more, that in the mouth of two or three witnesses every word may be established. (Matthew 18:16)

The charge to the Christian is to be a peacemaker. This is so different from what we are taught, what we have observed, and what our emotions dictate to us. We are captives of wrong thinking. The right thinking is to get past all the emotional fluff and hang-ups and to get back to our fellowship with the Lord. The Word tells us that our prayers are hindered when we are at odds with our spouses (1 Peter 3:7) and that our offerings are not acceptable to God when we are in contention with one another (Matthew 5:23–24). Can anything in the Bible be any clearer as to how we are to live our lives? After all, what are the two great commandments? To love God with

86

all your heart, soul, and mind, and to love others as you love yourself (Matthew 22:36–40).

So there you stand, aggrieved, having tried discussing the matter privately one-on one with the vilan, only to be rejected. What are you to do? Verse 16 does not instruct you to give up on this brother or to go tell everyone else your side of the story behind his back. To the contrary, it exhorts you to continue to resolve the matter privately in a series of rising progression. The next step is to take two or three witnesses to make certain that the words spoken are earnest and sincere to resolve the matter—for the benefit of the individual and for the benefit of the Church—and to preserve peace and purity in the Church.

You must rise to a higher calling. You have been charged with the responsibility to rectify this matter. That may seem unfair, but any other approach would result in one person winning and the other losing. Do you want your partner to be a loser? No, of course not. This person is your spouse, your friend, your partner, or, if there is no other way to describe them, this person is your brother or sister in Christ. This person is an equal heir in eternity with you and with Christ. If all else fails, you are to forgive and continue in prayer so that you are not burdened with the guilt and sin the situation brings. You are a winner because you have stayed aligned with Christ, and you have been the hope for healing in your relationship. Now, that's being a winner.

Always in Remembrance: *2 Peter 1:15*

1. *Christians are charged to be* _____.

2. *We are* _____ *of wrong thinking.*

3. *Right* _____ *is tracking in fellowship with the Lord.*

4. *Men's prayers are* _____ *when there are unresolved issues with wives.*

5. *Our offerings are not* _____ *to God when we are in contention with another.*

6. *We are to* _____ *others as we love ourselves.*

7. *One responds to a misunderstanding by first* _____ *it with the other person.*

8. *There is a specified escalation in the Church by which to* _____ *a conflict.*

9. *The Word prescribes having two or three* _____ *along to discuss the matter after meeting privately.*

10. *Resolving conflicts quickly preserves* _____ *in the Church.*

The Concept of a Witness

Higher Ground Principle # 18

Find a qualified Christian to help resolve a matter.

> Whoso killeth any person, the murderer shall be put
> to death by the mouth of witnesses: but *one witness*
> *shall not testify* against any person to cause him to die.
> (Numbers 35:30)

A witness is a powerful source to rely on for conviction. The Bible speaks to the severity of this by requiring that there be no less than two witnesses who speak forth on a matter. For that reason, the character of the witness always comes into contention, presuming that a witness should be one of good character, honest, and of integrity. In the Church, there are many individuals who can assist in resolving a matter between believers, but there are many more who are not qualified and whose character should be questioned. You do not want to turn your personal issues over to those who are uninstructed or inexperienced in counseling lest they cause you to lose objectivity and arrive at wrong conclusions that hurt the relationship rather than restore it. When bringing forth a matter that occurred in public, if there is to be any witnesses, there should be at least two objective and uninterested parties brought forth. Witnesses should only be utilized in the most severe of circumstances and as a matter of last resort. The practice of involving witnesses is not recommended unless absolutely necessary since it tends toward escalation of the issue and broadening the number of people involved.

> At the mouth of *two witnesses, or three witnesses,* shall
> he that is worthy of death be put to death; but at the
> mouth of one witness he shall not be put to death.
> The hands of the witnesses shall be first upon him to
> put him to death, and afterward the hands of all the
> people. So thou shalt put the evil away from among
> you. (Deuteronomy 17:6–7)

I wanted to examine in the verse above the question of integrity of the witness. Such a person must be so sure of what they are attesting to that the law requires them to be first to strike the accused in the case of a death sentence. Consider before you agree to be a witness for someone else that in God's view your hand is the first to fall upon the accused. Other scriptures on witnesses include the following:

> It is also written in your law, that the testimony of two men is true. I am one that bear witness of myself, and the Father that sent me beareth witness of me. (John 8:17–18)

> This is the third *time* I am coming to you. In the mouth of two or three witnesses shall every word be established. (2 Corinthians 13:1)

> Dare any of you, having a matter against another, go to law before the unjust, and not before the saints? Do ye not know that the saints shall judge the world? and if the world shall be judged by you, are ye unworthy to judge the smallest matters? Know ye not that we shall judge angels? how much more things that pertain to this life? If then ye have judgments of things pertaining to this life, *set them to judge who are least esteemed in the church*. I speak to your shame. Is it so, that there is not a wise man among you? no, not one that shall be able to judge between his brethren? But brother goeth to law with brother, and that before the unbelievers. Now therefore there is utterly a fault among you, because ye go to law one with another. *Why do ye not rather take wrong? why do ye not rather suffer yourselves to be defrauded?* Nay, ye do wrong, and defraud, and that your brethren. (1 Corinthians 6:1–8)

There is an alternative spoken of here: you can drop the entire matter. Why suffer more contention and disruption in your life over a single matter, especially one that pits you against another believer especially if it's someone you have a relationship with? Going to secular courts puts you in great jeopardy. In the Church, even the least esteemed is better qualified to judge than the most competent secular judge, and if these judges were to attend Church, they would be the least esteemed in the Church.

The witnesses are to be two or three disinterested parties, persons of some renown and respectability who can also reason the situation impartially with the opponent. Other believers or elders in the Church would be ideal. Do not take your posse or best friends who are coming along to stick up for you, and whatever else you may do, keep your family out of it. A brother in the Church is more likely to listen to reason from others than from you at this particular time. Let the witnesses be both arbitrators and keepers of the mental record of the proceedings. What if the brother refuses to listen to reason from the witnesses? Can you tell him off? No!

> And if he shall neglect to hear them, tell it unto the church: but if he neglect to hear the church, let him be unto thee as an heathen man and a publican. (Matthew 18:17)

There is yet another step that needs to be taken: bring the matter to the Church. This does not mean you get out on the pulpit and tell the congregation what an awful person your adversary is. In fact, any time there is a dispute between two persons, the matter should be handled privately among the fewest number of people possible. In the Church, this is of prime importance, because it resists the forces of division within and among the members of the Church. Remember that in the Church we want to aspire to peace and purity.

To tell it to the Church is to bring the matter privately to an elder or to the pastor. When a respected elder or the pastor applies the principles of the Word to the matter (2 Timothy 3:16–17) and if the person refuses to resolve it, then he is to be to you as are other people outside the Church. At this point, we are not just talking about arbitrating the matter. We are speaking about your obedience to God's Word by renewing your mind and refreshing your soul. You need to have your heart cleansed and find a new conviction as the Word of God ministers to your soul. The conviction you are to seek is for God's blessing into your adversary's life so that his heart may change and a blessing be received to prosper the two of you.

Treating him as a heathen or tax collector is an interesting concept worthy of discussing. Some have argued that this means you are now free to take this person to the authorities to keep him from causing you further harm or to recover losses or damages under civil law. Others contend that it means you should break off any friendship or closeness with this person and cease any further dealings. These certainly are arguments or acceptable compromises, but I have not found a biblical basis for such reasoning.

Remember, we are to apply biblical principles to achieve godly living, and we are to be like Christ. What would He have done in a situation like this? What does the Word say? It tells us to treat the person as we would a stranger, and the Word provides the recipe for the treatment of strangers.

> Thou shalt neither vex a stranger, nor oppress him: for ye were strangers in the land of Egypt. (Exodus 22:21)

> Let brotherly love continue. Be not forgetful to entertain strangers: for thereby some have entertained angels unawares. (Hebrews 13:1–2)

In these words, there is tremendous power and authority given into your hands. What if you had the power and authority to throw this person who has harmed you in prison? Wouldn't you want to give him what he has coming to him? Of course you would. That is our nature, to get even and extract vengeance by our own means. But let us consider God's justice.

> Brethren, if any of you do err from the truth, and one convert him; Let him know, that he which converteth

the sinner from the error of his way shall save a soul from death, and shall hide a multitude of sins. (James 5:19–20)

Verily I say unto you, Whatsoever ye shall bind on earth shall be bound in heaven: and whatsoever ye shall loose on earth shall be loosed in heaven. Again I say unto you, That if two of you shall agree on earth as touching any thing that they shall ask, it shall be done for them of my Father which is in heaven. For where two or three are gathered together in my name, there am I in the midst of them. (Matthew 18:18–20)

The Lord vested much power and authority in you. You can bind (like entering into a contract) in His name or commit to something on His behalf, and He will honor your call in Heaven. He also wants you to be in agreement with others around you. He says that in the company of two or three, when you ask in His name, His Father shall do it. Consider that God's purpose is to achieve salvation for as many people as possible, and Jesus's endeavor is to get as many as possible through the gates into the Kingdom of God for His Father. With this understanding in your grasp, would you be inclined to think that God has in any way given you the latitude to inflict harm on another person? He would prefer that you pray for others to seek repentance and that you forgive and look past each other's faults. The Lord has entrusted you with great responsibility and that's why He asks much of you. The tenderness and understanding you show to those who've harmed you complies with the Lord's expectation.

But he that knew not, and did commit things worthy of stripes, shall be beaten with few stripes. For *unto whomsoever much is given, of him shall be much* required: and to whom men have committed much, of him they will ask the more (Luke 12:48)

Always in Remembrance: 2 Peter 1:15

1. A matter can be _____ altogether if one so desires.

2. Going to secular court puts you in grave _____.

3. Respectable Church members of renown can reason _____ with both parties.

4. An aggrieved person is more likely to listen to _____ from others.

5. Resolving a matter between brethren off sets the forces _____ in the Church.

6. Telling it to the Church is to _____ the matter to the pastor or an elder.

7. We are to _____ biblical principles to achieve godly living.

8. You should _____ for forgiveness and repentance of any who cause you harm.

Scripture Reference:
Matthew 18:16; 1 Peter 3; Matthew 5:23–24; Numbers 35:30; Deuteronomy 17:6–7; John 8:17–18; 2 Corinthians 13:1; 1 Corinthians 6:1–8; Matthew 18:17; Exodus 22:21; Hebrews 13:1–2; James 5:19–20; Matthew 18:18–20; Proverbs 11:14; Luke 12:48

XIII. Constraints for Relationships on Finances

Higher Ground Principle #19

Lord, free me from the love of $money and chain my heart to loving you and to loving my brother.

"A friend in deed is a friend in need" (Author unknown. This old adage is not taken from the Bible).

Finances have led to more ruin in relationships and in the Church than have issues associated with sex. Money is the popular term for describing finances in relationships. In general, people are willing to compromise on most things, but not on $money. *(I've used the term $Money to signify the illicit love of money and to differentiate it from the functional purpose of money that is not tied to sin.)* $Money is a root that digs deep into the fiber of our society and is used as the chief measure for one's ability to survive, thrive, and enjoy life's pleasures. $Money is the irresistible magnetic force that compels us to do strange things, often contrary to our better judgment and contrary to our walk of faith. The end result of our romance with $money usually concludes in disappointment, breakups, or disaster.

> For the love of money is the root of all evil: which while some coveted after, they have erred from the faith, and pierced themselves through with many sorrows. (1 Timothy 6:10)

Our sense of $money is to want more of it and to fight to keep what we have, because it provides us with a sense of security and independence. $Money creates a passionate sense of comfort and security centered on the power to buy with cash or credit the things that validate our sense of social status. If you stop and think about it, this is a sad view. Our message to each other is to place the value of human worth, in comparison to one another, according to how we compare financially.

In this segment, we will examine the concept of relationships to money and how to relate to others in your life when it comes to money. This issue is pervasive and runs deep into our way of life. It deprives us of the opportunity to value one another on the same terms as the Lord Jesus values us.

Overcoming Love of $Money

Each of us who covets our relationship with $money has a misplaced love. It cannot be said that money should not be sought after as a means of satisfying our needs. If we replace our reliance on God's sufficiency with reliance on $money we have in the bank or credit we hold in our cards, then the belief that $money can buy us everything will engulf us. We are flawed in our expectation for deliverance, and we put our families and our lives in jeopardy. God, in His ever-knowing wisdom, identified the tendency for man to love $money as a fault and offered a way to overcome this enslaving predicament with $money.

> And all the tithe of the land, whether of the seed of
> the land, or of the fruit of the tree, is the LORD's: it
> is holy unto the LORD. (Leviticus 27:30)

In making the declaration that the first tenth of all belongs to Him, God sets in place a pattern to release man from the bondage and sin of covetousness for $money. If we start to pattern ourselves and to teach our children the habit of giving that first ten percent of our increase, the value of the remaining ninety percent will be multiplied. We will build a mental barrier of separation from money that later in life will prevent us from becoming obsessed with the love of $money. Our faithful obligation is to honor God by meeting His every requirement, tithing being among the highest on the list. Subsequently, we will build a pattern of unselfish giving that will be unparalleled to any covetousness for $money or things.

It is said that breaking up is hard to do, and for many adult believers, breaking up our relationship with $money is next to impossible. You can either go at it cold turkey by closing your mind to the perceived loss and trusting God once and for all—I say trusting God once and for all, because you will see His benevolent hand at work in your life so that you are never without life's necessities from that day forth. The other option is to tithe sporadically as need for God's intervention in your life's affairs comes up and His faithfulness will affirm this faith and trust within you. Or you can simply go on living your presumed Christian way of life in total denial and self deceit, and not see the grand works of God manifested. Those who live this way fail to prove God and live their lives in doubt and turmoil.

> For if there be first a willing mind, it is accepted according to that a man hath, and not according to that he hath not. (2 Corinthians 8:12)

$Money in Your Relationship

You can sarcastically conclude that the way to avoid conflict when it comes to money is to not lend or give any of your own. This may solve your problem, but it does not address the calling in God's Word.

> For, brethren, ye have been called unto liberty; only use not liberty for an occasion to the flesh, but by love serve one another. For all the law is fulfilled in one word, even in this; Thou shalt love thy neighbour as thyself. (Galatians 5:13–14)

Here is the problem: we are to serve one another by love. If we withhold the world's goods from our brethren in need, how then can we live by this rule? Does it mean I give my money to others or lend it, undeserving though they may be? Who is to judge when it is the right situation and when it is not? What does the Word have to say regarding this? Let us examine it.

Acts 4:34-35 details how the the believers unselfishly sold their excess possessions, brought the proceeds to the Church, and divided among the people according to need. The most impressive thing to see is how the people were moved in their hearts to do the thing that at any other time would have been very arduous to do. They sold their lands and their extra stuff to give it willingly (and I might add, lovingly) for the benefit of others who had not even asked.

What happened in chapter four of Acts? What took place to cause this marvelous and unsolicited universal turn of events?

We can see from the record that prayer was involved, a very deep and intense prayer that shook the house. Then, the Holy Ghost came upon them, and all of a sudden, people were doing the unthinkable. They sold their lands and possessions to give to the poor. You should bear in mind that prior to this inspired motivation, these folks had been greatly moved by events surrounding the miracle performed by Peter and John on the lame man. Not to mention, the turnabout from the usual harsh treatment, punishment, and imprisonment of the saints by the Sanhedrin to a passive treatment of Peter and John.

The believers highly exalted God and the Lord Jesus, in whose name they were forbidden to speak. They all got together and prayed. You may be saying to yourself, "Good for them, but what does this have to do with me? What does this have to do with me and my love of $money?"

It's all about seeing the magnificence of God, His hand of providence and His eminent rule over man. It's about understanding that God wants you to put Him first, before anything else in your life, and that you show Him you have properly put Him first by relinquishing your hold on material things, including $money, and relying totally on Him. Do you trust God to provide for your every need in every situation?

Your relationship with others will be greatly enlarged if you can view it as not dependent on resources, but dependent on God. If you can surrender your fear of being without and together with your friends, spouse, children, employees, and others rely on God to make life's necessary provisions available to you, then you will prosper together beyond measure. God challenges you to come into His presence together in prayer in your relationship, being of one mind and of one accord as to your needs, wants, and desires, and to allow Him to fulfill the desires of your heart. But, should you come divided in purpose or divided in intent, your benefit will be at best a smaller portion of all that would have otherwise been available if you had come united together as one.

You must approach your relationship not as two separate finances, but as one. You are not two households, but one. The details of how it works, though complicated in your understanding, must be worked out by you in the sight of God. You can start by setting time aside and preparing a total and complete disclosure of income and expenses. Begin to work at this today. Take the initiative. Be the first. Take the lead. Learn to separate yourself from the love of $money, and unite yourself with your loved one, or if in business, unite yourself with those whom you have chosen to partner with. And most important, partner with God.

Whether a business partnership or marriage, the relationship must express with clear definition each one's role and the percent of contribution to the total of the goal. The percentage of your contribution in relationship to your ability is what matters in this case, not the amount contributed. You want to confirm to each other that you're making the adequate and required contribution toward achieving the goal. Are you both clear as to what each is expected to contribute to the financial goal of the relationship?

Always in Remembrance: *2 Peter 1:15*

1.   The _____ of $money is the root of all evil.

2.   The unchecked status of finances may lead to _____ in the relationship.

3.   Desire for $money can _____ us to do strange things.

4.   We use $money to _____ our social status.

5.   Your relationship with $money _____ your relationship with others.

6.   The tendency to love $money is a _____ in man.

7.   The first _____ of all belongs to God.

8.   We are to serve one another by _____, not by the value of our money.

9.   Surrender your _____ to God, and allow Him to fulfill the desires of your heart.

10. Approach your relationship not as two _____ finances, but as one.

Scripture Reference:

1 Timothy 6:10; Leviticus 27:30; 2 Corinthians 8:12; Galatians 5:13–14; Acts 4:34

XIV. How Much Forgiveness, Lord?

Higher Ground Principle # 20

Have unlimited forgiveness for others as God has for you.

The problem we encounter with forgiveness is that there is no gray area to dwell in. Forgiveness is absolute and complete. For example, love, according to the Word, is an absolute condition to be fulfilled. Yet, you may choose to love according to how you feel or how you perceive that you have been made to feel. In your own mind, love is measured in varying degrees, depending on how you feel about a person. You reason that you either love someone a little or that you are working on loving them. So, your love is conditional, and worse than that, your love is inconsistent from person to person.

One way of establishing consistency in loving others is by your willingness to forgive. You may be more willing to forgive one person over another or one trespass over another. Yet, the requirement is to forgive all.

Forgiveness does not afford you the luxury to fantasize about it. It is absolute, just as love is absolute. You cannot reason varying degrees of forgiveness in your mind, because it just does not work that way. If you can't bring yourself to completely forgive, it is probably because it does not fit into your way of thinking. However, you are required by God to have complete and total forgiveness of others, and if you fail to comply with this, you know that you have fallen short of God's commandment. You cannot change God's commandment, so you must change your way of thinking. You can't skate around this and say you have forgiven a little. This might be enough to look good in the eyes of others, but not in the eyes of God. You may be cool with your friends, but you are not cool with Jesus if you have not forgiven all.

This is the question that Peter asks Jesus, and a question most of us rarely ask, though we need to ask it more often, "How many times am I to forgive someone?". Your position on forgiveness may be not to forgive than it is to being forgiving. You want to see repentance on the part of the aggressor before you offer up any semblance of forgiveness. You want to hear those two words, "I'm sorry." When you finally do accept to do the Christian requirement to forgive, your reluctance to be forgiving might result in a conversation with the Lord similar to the encounter He had with Peter.

The Lord:	**You are to forgive.**
You:	Lord, I will forgive him this one time, if he promises never to do that again. That's all I'm willing to do.
The Lord:	**No. That's not good enough.**
You:	Okay, Lord. I'll forgive him seven times.
The Lord:	**Ha, ha, ha! Seven times?**
You:	All right, Lord. I'll forgive him seven times seven times!
The Lord:	**No, my child. Try at least seventy times seven. How about if you forgive him 490 times? Then come back and talk to me about it.**

Until you have fulfilled the will of the Lord, there is little or nothing you can say to Him or ask of Him with any right of expectation. You may find that you pray often over the situation, and the right result doesn't come. Why? It doesn't come because you have yet to forgive in your heart.

> Then came Peter to him, and said, Lord, how oft shall my brother sin against me, and I forgive him? Till seven times? Jesus saith unto him, *I say not unto thee, Until seven times: but, Until seventy times seven.* (Matthew 18:21–22)

In the Kingdom of God, there is no limit placed on forgiveness. Forgiveness is always in style and expected on demand. (A checking account is called a demand deposit. This means that the bank must give up the money whenever the owner of the account asks for it, on demand.) Forgiveness is a demand account of the Lord's. It is not you who demands forgiveness from the other person; rather, it is the Lord who demands forgiveness from you of others. The reason He can demand this forgiveness is expressed in the following Parable. (*Parables – are stories, especially those of Jesus, told to provide a vision of life, especially life in God's Kingdom. Parable means a putting alongside for purposes of comparison and new understanding. Parables utilize (word) pictures such as metaphors or similes and frequently extend them into a brief story to make a point or disclosure. Holman, Bible Dictionary, p. 1071*).

> Therefore is the kingdom of heaven likened unto a certain king, which would take account of his servants. And when he had begun to reckon, one was brought unto him, which *owed him ten thousand talents.* (Matthew 18:23–33)

Ten thousand is a very large sum. It should cause us to want to explore the context of such a large number. Also, what is a talent? Surely this is not referring to *American Idol.* Whatever a talent is, this servant owed his master 10,000 of them.

A talent is a measure of about 75 pounds, as we would understand it. One talent is worth about 750 ounces of silver. A talent has also been defined as a measure equivalent to more than fifteen years labor for one worker. This guy owed 10,000 talents. It would take 150,000 years of labor or 7,500,000 ounces of silver to pay it back. That's a total of 468,750 pounds of silver or 1,000 laborers working for fifteen years. The debt was enormous, and it was unlikely that the servant would be able to pay it off.

But forasmuch as he had not to pay, his lord commanded him to be sold, and his wife, and children, and all that he had, and payment to be made. The servant therefore fell down, and worshipped him, saying, Lord, have patience with me, and I will pay thee all. Then the lord of that servant was moved with compassion, and loosed him, and *forgave him the debt.*

…But the same servant went out, and found one of his fellowservants, which *owed him an hundred pence…*

100 pence is worth 1/8th of an ounce of silver or about one day's wages. How could this possibly compare to 150,000 years of labor? The comparison is around 54.8 million to one.

…and he laid hands on him, and took him by the throat, saying, Pay me that thou owest. And his fellowservant fell down at his feet, and besought him, saying, Have patience with me, and I will pay thee all. And he would not: but went and cast him into prison, till he should pay the debt.

How awful for this servant not to have learned the lesson taught him by his master and followed his master's example of forgiveness. Wouldn't the master have been proud of his servant and gratified that he had done the right thing for his servant? Wouldn't he have been happy that his example was well received and that it might have started a virtuous cycle among his servants, his household, his neighborhood, and throughout the entire land? What a terrible missed opportunity by this greedy and selfish person to please his master and bless his brethren.

> So when his fellowservants saw what was done, they were very sorry, and came and told unto their lord all that was done. Then his lord, after that he had called him, said unto him, O *thou wicked servant*, I forgave thee all that debt, because thou desiredst me:

> *Shouldest not thou also have had compassion on thy fellowservant, even as I had pity on thee?*

When you fail to forgive you are nothing less than a wicked servant. Can you see now why so few of us, if any, are ever worthy of receiving anything from the Lord? He has given you a rich benefit in that you do not have to pay the penalty of sin. You have been pardoned completely. Jesus is not charging you for the forgiveness you have received. Jesus made payment for you by the sacrifice of His innocent life for you when you were the least worthy to have been forgiven. You owe it to the Lord to forgive others as He forgave you. The trespasses of others against you do not compare with your trespass against God.

What can you learn from this parable? It's that you had better forgive. It is in your best interest to forgive if you want to be accounted for obedience to the Lord.

> And his lord was wroth, and delivered him to the tormentors, till he should pay all that was due unto him. *So likewise shall my heavenly Father do also unto you, if ye from your hearts forgive not every one his brother their trespasses.* (Matthew 18:34–35)

Reality can be very harsh. Verse 35 leaves no wiggle room. It says "likewise shall My Heavenly Father do also unto you." This is a promise with every potential for fulfillment. You will be delivered to the tormentors for failure to forgive. You have been forgiven for so much, yet you find it so difficult to forgive someone else. Carefully consider the consequences.

> Whoso stoppeth his ears at the cry of the poor, he also shall cry himself, but shall not be heard. (Proverbs 21:13)

> And forgive us our debts, as we forgive our debtors. (Matthew 6:12)

> For he *shall have judgment without mercy, that hath shewed no mercy*, and mercy rejoiceth against judgment. (James 2:13)

It is remarkable how forgiveness operates in your life. If you are unforgiving, then you are unnecessarily laden with a heavy burden. You can remove this burden by your own free will desire to do so. If you are laden down with too may burdens, you will become sluggish, tired, and unable to move. This is a spiritual law, and the consequences are manifested in your spiritual life. Perhaps you are that one person that really loves God and wants so much to do His will. You want to have fellowship with likeminded believers and be a significant part of the household, but you encounter every difficulty and barrier in getting to church—waking on time for fellowship meetings, having to overcome obstacles in order to get to prayer night, and so on. If you should be the one having these kinds of experiences, you might want to consider that it may be a spiritual matter that needs to be dealt with. It might just be that you are too overloaded with sin and guilt and overwhelmed by the weight of your unforgiving heart. Let it go. Let go and let God do what is best for you. Forgive.

Let the Word of God speak to your heart. If you want to have good and meaningful godly relationships, your heart must be prepared to partake with them. If you are not weighted down, then you will be able to freely enjoy your relationship.

> Cast thy burden upon the LORD, and he shall sustain thee: he shall never suffer the righteous to be moved. (Psalm 55:22)

Always in Remembrance: 2 Peter 1:15

1. There is no _____ area to dwell in when it comes to forgiveness.

2. We are often _____ to forgive others.

3. The Lord _____ that you forgive others.

4. Forgiveness may start a _____ cycle in your relationship.

5. Not forgiving _____ you down with heavy burdens.

6. You can freely _____ your relationship if your heart is not weighted down.

Scripture Reference:
Matthew 18:21–22; Matthew 18:23–33; Matthew 18:34–35; Proverbs 21:13; Matthew 6:12; James 2:13; Psalms 55:22

XV. A Soft Answer Turns away Wrath, and Iron Does Sharpen Iron

Higher Ground Principle # 21

Measure your words and avoid offending others.

There are two biblical principles you must uphold that will affect your relationship positively, or if ignored will cause negativity to set in. If you err in these two marvelous biblical principles, your misunderstanding will have an adverse affect on your relationship. When properly applied, however, these are two powerful principles to live by and from which to harvest fruit in the relationship. They are spiritual laws that work spiritually in your relationship to accomplish their purpose.

> A soft answer turneth away wrath: but grievous words stir up anger. (Proverbs 15:1)

What is a soft answer for?

This principle has one purpose and that is to quench fiery buildup in an argument. Simply put, lower your tone, respond with a kind word, and keep from shooting out darts of retort that infuriate the other person. The effect will be to quiet down the situation until cooler heads prevail and you have a better climate for handling the issue. The purpose in applying this principle is never to teach the other person a lesson or to improve upon their social skills, but rather to bring peace.

The concept of iron sharpening iron

> Iron sharpeneth iron; so a man sharpeneth the countenance of his friend. (Proverbs 27:17)

On the other hand, iron does sharpen iron. I have the distinguished job of sharpening the knives in the kitchen. This is a job that I perform, and when ever I get around to it I rarely do it well. One of my daughters is quick to criticize. She can't understand why our knives are constantly being sharpened, but always seem dull. To that I would like to say, "Maybe it's because we cook with them often, unlike other people." However, that would not be a soft answer. That would be a hard and provoking answer, and the Word says we should not provoke our children to wrath. I think that includes our adult children too.

For the knives in the kitchen to get sharpened, they must be rubbed on a file, flint, metal or stone to sharpen them. If rubbed against a sponge, there would be gentle contact, but it would not result in the knife getting sharp. So it is in our lives. Sometimes the Word of God hits us like an anvil dropping on a foot. It hurts, and it pains us to listen, to accept it, and then to obey it. It rarely fails in marriage counseling that when the wife is told to submit to her husband, the hackles go up. When angry or disappointed, wives hear what the Word says in Ephesians 5:22, that wives are to submit, and they reject it. They say, "Oh, no. I'm not going to submit to him!"

By now, the husbands are usually grinning from cheek to cheek, until I read further in verse 25 where it says that husbands are to love their wives as Jesus Christ loves the church. That definitely brings the husband down from grin heaven. There response is, "Oh, no! I don't have to love her if she is mean to me or if she doesn't show love and respect to me!" (What he may really mean is, "I don't have to love her if she is not fulfilling my desires.")

In either case, the Word is like iron. If the recipient were made of iron, he or she would allow the Word to rub him or her down until they get sharp regarding the matter. The fact is that when either or both spouses apply the respective principle without constraint, the result is outstanding. The marital relationship soon turns to a positive one. When rubbed against him, the iron in the Word sharpens the iron in the man in a positive and constructive way, and the heart of the man is prepared to obey and to do the will of God, no matter how painful it may be.

God uses the iron of His ways to chastise men and women of God and to sharpen them up so that they come to their senses. The prodigal son sharpened up only after he had spent all his inheritance and was compelled to steal slop from pigs to feed his hunger. Only then did he realize how much was provided for the lowliest servant in his father's house and how the abundance of food was of much better quality than pig slop. The chastening sharpened him up.

> And the younger of them said to his father, Father, give me the portion of goods that falleth to me. And he divided unto them his living. And not many days after the younger son gathered all together, and took his journey into a far country, and there wasted his substance with riotous living. And when he had spent all, there arose a mighty famine in that land; and he began to be in want. And he went and joined himself to a citizen of that country; and he sent him into his fields to feed swine. And he would fain have filled his belly with the husks that the swine did eat: and no man gave unto him. And when he came to himself, he said, How many hired servants of my father's have bread enough and to spare, and I perish with hunger! I will arise and go to my father, and will say unto him, Father, I have sinned against heaven, and before thee. (Luke 15:12–18)

Neither hypocrisy nor harshness makes you sharp:

Some people are always politically correct. They never say anything that can be mistaken for criticism, nor do they confront their friends. People like this may not want to hurt other people's feelings, or they may simply desire to remain agreeable to others so that they are liked and thought of in a positive light. This is hypocrisy, and it should never be tolerated, especially in a relationship. A relationship requires that each person is honest and truthful without employing words or tactics that issue out in the form of an insult, hurtfulness, or harshness toward their partner. Some may grasp at the opportunity to unload things they have had on their chests under the guise of positive criticism, but that is not acceptable either, because it is insincere and lacks in integrity. So, the sharpening of iron in the person requires truth and honesty in place of hypocrisy and integrity and sincerity in the place of a guise for dumping on your partner. A healthy relationship is built on THIS.

A relationship is not required to always be a bed of roses all the time. Being truthful, honest, and sincere can cause friction and give off some friendly sparks from time to time. If handled properly, constructive criticism is exactly the type of iron sharpening iron that is needed, the sharpening of each other's countenance in the relationship. The end result of this controlled and well-placed abrasion causes improvement in the quality of the persons in the relationship. It sharpens up and improves the quality of the relationship. Jesus, it can be said, roughed Peter up several times. One time, He told Peter to get behind Him, Satan. Matthew 16:23 At another time, as He lifted Peter from sinking in the water, He told Peter he was of little faith. Matthew 14:31 These were strong words, but they sharpened the rough edges of the fisherman who became a fisher of men. After the Lord's ascension Peter rose up and assumed spiritual leadership for the trembling disciples who previously were locked up in an upper room for fear of what the leaders of the Jews and the local authorities might do to them. Peter's boldness and leadership in the Gospel can be seen throughout the book of Acts and the following epistles, including the books he wrote (Acts 2:14–40).

Always in Remembrance: *2 Peter 1:15*

1. *A soft answer to an angered partner is for the purpose of bringing about _____ .*

2. *It is not necessary to have hard and _____ responses in your conversation.*

3. *Accepting the _____ in God's Word can be very confronting.*

4. *God's unbending ways are like iron to _____ and sharpen a man.*

5. *Sharpening from God is to bring us back to our _____*

6. *_____ in a relationship should not be tolerated.*

7. *A relationship can have _____ but constructive confrontation.*

8. *Well placed constructive _____ improves the quality of a relationship.*

Scripture Reference:
Proverbs 15:1; Proverbs 27:17; Ephesians 5:22, 25; Matthew 16:23; Matthew 14:31; Acts 2:14–40

XVI. The Perfect Partnership

Higher Ground Principle # 22

Form a perfect partnership in your relationship as did Jesus with God and as Jesus desires to have with you.

The culmination of a healthy relationship is the perfect partnership. On earth, this is a rare sighting, if actually ever seen. We have more examples of poor and dysfunctional partnerships than perfect partnerships. There is only one place to turn for a respite from what we see all around us. The relationship between God and Jesus provides the keys to unlocking the secrets of the perfect relationship. This is what Building Blocks for Relationships has attempted to describe. Building blocks are fundamental in children's learning. They teach that you can firmly support a third block by placing it atop two other blocks laid side by side. Applying this enlarges our understanding for constructing a building with the concepts of sound footings, solid foundations and weight bearing walls. These serve the same purpose as truth, honesty, integrity and sincerity (THIS), if used as the basic blocks for building a relationship.

God loves Jesus, and Jesus loves God. They have clarity with regards to who is in charge and who is the ultimate decision maker; there is no doubt between them. However, despite His prevailing authority, God will not violate Jesus' free will to exercise His own will upon his choosing. God would respect Him for any choice Jesus would make.

> And he said, Abba, Father, all things are possible unto thee; take away this cup from me: nevertheless not what I will, but what thou wilt. (Mark 14:36)

Relying on the experience of His perfect relationship with His Father, Jesus tells us to take His yoke. In simple English, He would say, "Partner up with me. I know the ins and outs of how to have and maintain a perfect relationship. Let's model a partnership after the example of My Father and Me." Consider the words spoken in the following scripture.

> All things are delivered unto me of my Father: and no man knoweth the Son, but the Father; neither knoweth any man the Father, save the Son, and he to whomsoever the Son will reveal him. Come unto me, all ye that labour and are heavy laden, and I will give you rest. Take my yoke upon you, and learn of me; for I am meek and lowly in heart: and ye shall find rest unto your souls. For my yoke is easy, and my burden is light. (Matthew 11:27–30)

Jesus describes the intimacy of His relationship with God. He says that no man knows either Him or Me the way that He knows Me and the way that I know Him. We have something special. We have a healthy and robust relationship. We have the perfect partnership. Jesus appeals to our understanding, in a sense, by coaxing us into wanting to partner with Him. Who among us does not labor day after day, sometimes over the same thing? We are heavy laden, weighted down with the issues of life, with our emotional battles, and with our crippled relationships. All of mankind is in need of rest. Jesus promises rest to all who labor and are weighted down, if they will come to Him.

Let us suppose that a very wealthy person knocked on your door one day and said, "Here is a contract, a partnership agreement.

I promise to put up all the money that you will ever need to do business with me. Moreover, you don't have to do much of the work. I will take care of that for us. What I want you to do is just keep me company, be loyal, and do what I ask of you. I promise not to abuse our relationship or ask you to do any wrong." What would you say? You would say, "Yes, yes, yes. My ship finally came in. I'm finally getting the break I deserve." You would throw your shoulders back and be proud of yourself. You would stumble and fall running for a pen to sign the partnership agreement.

Jesus's offer is for you to partner with Him. If you become His partner He will take the load off your back and give you the light chores to do. He will relieve you of the hardships of life and replace them with joy and prosperity. Once you partner with Jesus, you will transform and become like Him. It is at this point in your spiritual maturity that you will be able to extend yourself to others and build a relationship that is modeled after your relationship with the Lord. Your relationships on earth will include Him. You will form that three string cord which is not easily broken (Ecclesiastes 4:12b).

You will dwell in THIS: truth, honesty, integrity, and sincerity. You will weave the concepts of sanctification, sacrifice, substitution, submission, and survival of your relationship into your very fiber of life. You will be the driving force to work spiritual laws into your relationship, and the results will propel your relationship into a perfect partnership where soft words are spoken to take away wrath and where constructive criticism works to sharpen the partners and improve the quality of the relationship. You will be the catalyst in forming the perfect partnership on earth.

Always in Remembrance: *2 Peter 1:15*

1. A _____ relationship is the ultimate in making the perfect partnership.

2. Jesus has the _____ partnership with God.

3. By developing a relationship with Jesus, we construct a _____ for relationships on earth.

4. A perfect partnership enjoys intimacy and _____ in its core.

5. Partnership with Jesus brings _____ and prosperity into our lives.

6. Spiritual maturity allows us to _____ our relationship with God into our relationship with others.

Scripture Reference:
Mark 14:36; Matthew 11:27–30

XVII. A Lasting Finish

I have titled this study *Building Blocks for Relationships*. It is intended as a guide that gently imparts the godly purposes you should have in your relationship. This book is designed to offer you the opportunity to change how you perceive and approach your relationships with others. Every relationship can stand to change in some way in order for it to improve.

Among my objectives is to make you aware of the rudiments that comprise a godly relationship in the hope that you elect to adopt the Christian biblical principles that will affect positive change in your relationships now and throughout your life. This is a guide book to spiritual laws that work the same all the time, and work the same for everyone, if the prescribed conditions are met. In that sense, it is a rulebook that applies in every case and will guide you back to God and His Word regarding how to relate to others. A successful relationship will exist when two people adhere to and apply Christian principles. A healthy solution may be had if at first only one person is willing to apply the principles and live by these godly standards. My desire is that you continue in prayer and trust in our Lord Jesus Christ, the Messiah, and through Him, fortify your understanding of how to improve your relationship through godliness. I hope that you will use this study as a building block in your quest and pursuit for a relationship at a higher spiritual and godly place in your life.

An example of a pure and perfect relationship is provided in God, the Father, and His son, Jesus. Either one could have tried to negatively influence, lie to, or deceive the other on something they did not intend to do. They could have elected to hypocritically handle their interrelationship without truth, honesty, integrity, or sincerity (THIS) in their intentions or communication. This is far from being the case. As a matter of fact, we have no better example of a relationship than that of God and Jesus. Like Jesus, we should also endeavor to build our personal relationship with God based on THIS. Our relationship with Jesus is to be established on the same principles as is our relationship with God. In Jesus, we have one more requirement to live up to, and that is to obey His commandments as were given to Him by God. Both God and Jesus have already proven their integrity to you. It is up to you to prove your integrity in a relationship with them. In proving your integrity to God you will learn that you can experience a similar joy in your earthly relationship through the application of the teachings found in the Word. Experiencing THIS with people is what prepares you to experience THIS with God. How you relate to others around you, people that you see and touch, is the true measure of how you relate to God, whom you can't see or touch.

The godly relationship begins by the Lord relieving you of your heavy burdens, the things that weigh you down in life, which He takes on as His own burdens in place of you. This occurs when you accept His yoke (when you commit to hitching up with Him), then His promise of rest unto your soul is realized. By giving your burdens of life over to Him, you are freed of the weighty matters in your life, and you replace those weighty matters with His principles as you apply them in your life. (Please consult your pastor for details on how to make this transition in your spiritual relationship. I am certain your pastor will be blessed to help.)

The starting point for improving your earthly relationships or for starting up a new relationship is in the application of truth, honesty, integrity, and sincerity (THIS). Once you have begun a life pattern of basing your relationships on THIS, you will find applying the 5Ss (sanctification—a setting apart; sacrifice—giving up your preference; substitution—putting yourself in their place; submission—giving in to another's point of view; and survival—persevering in the relationship) simpler and easier to do. The Higher Ground Principles are summarized in the Appendix to provide a quick reference step by step spiritual concepts to apply in the areas of your relationship that need attention.

As you open your heart to God and the spiritual principles for relationships, you will also open your heart to your friends. When your relationship with god and the Lord are working well, your relationships with others will work well also. This will bring peace and rest into your life. Ponder these thoughts in light of the following words:

Matthew 11:28-30

Come unto me, all ye that labour and are heavy laden, and I will give you rest. Take my yoke upon you, and learn of me; for I am meek and lowly in heart: and ye shall find rest unto your souls. For my yoke is easy, and my burden is light.

APPENDIX: Answer Key

Always in Remembrance: *2 Peter 1:15*

Section II   page 19
Have THIS…

AIR
1. dealings
2. control
3. THIS
4. correct
5. work, truth
6. faith
7. spiritual
8. lying
9. judge
10. joy

Section III   page 25
What Constitutes…

AIR
1. others
2. purpose
3. consider
4. reason

5. clean
6. THIS
7. gain
8. now
9. failure
10. mutual

Section III   page 32
The 5 Ss

AIR
1. Sanctification
2. support
3. Sacrifice
4. substitution
5. Submission
6. survival

Section IV   page 37
Working to Build...

AIR
1. build
2. will
3. common
4. honor
5. conflict
6. poor
7. respect
8. right

Section V   page 42
Examining Faults...

AIR
1. decline
2. vicious

3. unwilling
4. listening
5. diffuse
6. emotional
7. guarded
8. built-up
9. together
10. sacrifices

Section VI   page 47
Building Success...

AIR
1. virtuous
2. positive
3. mind
4. emotions
5. nourish
6. decisions
7. repair
8. value

7. equipped
8. calm
9. affect

Section IX   page 61
The Salt of the Earth

AIR
1. peacemakers
2. salt
3. flavoring
4. good
5. lives
6. share

Section IX   page 64
The Light of the World

AIR
1. illuminate
2. daily
3. lead
4. light
5. hidden
6. God

Section IX   page 73
Ten Points of Light

AIR
1. honest
2. good
3. Obey
4. expectation
5. use
6. first
7. disrespect

8. love
9. Hold
10. Honor

Section X   page 77
Handling Those Who...

AIR
1. redeemed
2. right
3. reconciled
4. agree
5. straighten
6. avoid

Section XI   page 83
Handling Quarrels...

AIR
1. grieves
2. provokes
3. bullying
4. accusation
5. injurious
6. annoying

Section XI   page 85
Maintaining Good Relationships

AIR
1. attitude
2. simmer
3. defensive
4. control
5. Jesus
6. soft

Section XII   page 88
The Witness of the Church

AIR
1. peacemakers
2. captives
3. thinking
4. hindered
5. acceptable
6. love
7. discussing
8. resolve
9. witnesses
10. purity

Section XII   page 94
The Concept of a Witness

AIR
1. dropped
2. jeopardy
3. impartially
4. reason
5. division
6. bring
7. apply
8. pray

Section XIII   page 100
Constraints for Relationships

AIR
1. love
2. ruin
3. compel
4. validate
5. affects
6. fault

7. tenth
8. love
9. fears
10. separate

Section XIV   page 107
How Much Forgiveness...

AIR
1. grey
2. reluctant
3. demands
4. virtuous
5. weighs
6. enjoy

Section XV   page 112
A Soft Answer...

AIR
1. peace
2. provoking
3. truth
4. chastise
5. senses
6. Hypocrisy
7. friendly
8. criticism

Section XVI   page 116
The Perfect Partnership

AIR
1. healthy
2. perfect
3. model
4. loyalty
5. joy
6. extend

Higher Ground Principles

Workshop Exercises

We have prepared seven Workshop Exercises. Each one is designed for a specific user:

1. Woman/Wife
2. Employee
3. Employer
4. Child
5. Parent
6. Friend
7. Man/Husband

The exercises are designed for either group or individual use. The group exercise can be conducted at a meeting of a particular user group or in a breakout session for a larger diversified group. A round table discussion can be had after group participants have worked individually on their own worksheets, which may prove useful and encouraging. The exercise can be conducted by a couple at home to assist each other in learning more about biblical responsibilities, or to help each other to meet their biblical obligations.

The exercises are designed with selected scriptures that define the biblical principles and Christian qualities for each user group. The exercises ask that you read the scripture, review the biblical qualities it addresses, and annotate how you are applying it. If it's a quality you are not presently applying, then you are to define the action you are willing to take to apply the quality. You are encouraged to search the Bible for additional scriptures you may want to add.

Building Blocks for Relationships

Workshop Exercise # 1
(A Woman, A Wife)

Directions:

1. Search the selected verses and identify the biblical principles described. In your group session make a list of the principles found (20 minutes)

2. Privately identify the principles you are presently applying in your relationship as a woman or a wife. Briefly explain how you are fulfilling each principle. (10 minutes)

3. Identify the principles you are not fulfilling. Describe a brief plan for how you intend to fulfill them. Be prepared to share at your discretion. (10 minutes)

Bible Scripture	Biblical Qualities	Applying	Not Applying
Proverbs 31:10	-rare to find a virtuous wife -is of great value		
Proverbs 31:11	-earned her husband's trust -doesn't need to skim		
Proverbs 31:12	-is loyal to him -honors him		
Proverbs 31:13	-self-sufficient to do her housework		
Proverbs 31:14	-wise about finances		
Proverbs 31:15	-meets needs of the family		

Proverbs 31:16	-wise in business		
Proverbs 31:17	-is not afraid to do hard work		
Proverbs 31:18	-keeps herself looking well -does not pass out at night		
Proverbs 31:20	-is kind and giving		
Proverbs 31:23	-makes her husband proud		
Proverbs 31:25	-is covered in honor		
Proverbs 31:26	-is wise and careful about what she speaks		
Proverbs 31:31	-is revered by others		

Notes

Building Blocks for Relationships

Workshop Exercise # 2
(Employee)

Directions:
1. Search the selected verses and identify the biblical principles described. In your group session make a list of the principles found (20 minutes)

2. Privately identify the principles you are presently applying in your relationship as an employee. Briefly explain how you are fulfilling each principle. (10 minutes)

3. Identify the principles you are not fulfilling. Describe a brief plan for how you intend to fulfill them. Be prepared to share at your discretion. (10 minutes)

Bible Scripture	Biblical Qualities	Applying	Not Applying
Exodus 21.5	-faithfulness		
Ephesians 6.5	-obedience		
Colossians 3:22	-loyalty and professionalism		
I Timothy 6:1	-respect		
Titus 2.9	-desire to please		
1 Peter 2:18	-patience in hard times		

Notes

Building Blocks for Relationships

Workshop Exercise # 3
(Employer)

Directions:
1. Search the selected verses and identify the biblical principles described. In your group session make a list of the principles found (20 minutes)

2. Privately identify the principles you are presently applying in your relationship as an employer. Briefly explain how you are fulfilling each principle. (10 minutes)

3. Identify the principles you are not fulfilling. Describe a brief plan for how you intend to fulfill them. Be prepared to share at your discretion. (10 minutes)

Bible Scripture	Biblical Qualities	Applying	Not Applying
Deuteronomy 24.15	-prompt payment of wages		
Job 31:13–14	-consideration for employees		
Ephesians 6:9	-refrain from threats		
Colossians 4:1	-deal justly		

Notes

Building Blocks for Relationships

Workshop Exercise # 4
(Child)

Directions:

1. Search the selected verses and identify the biblical principles described. In your group session make a list of the principles found (20 minutes)

2. Privately identify the principles you are presently applying in your relationship as a child. Briefly explain how you are fulfilling each principle. (10 minutes)

3. Identify the principles you are not fulfilling. Describe a brief plan for how you intend to fulfill them. Be prepared to share at your discretion. (10 minutes)

Bible Scripture	Biblical Qualities	Applying	Not Applying
Psalms 34.11	-to fear the Lord		
Proverbs 10.1	-make parents glad		
Proverbs 20:11	-do pure and right works		
Proverbs 23.22	-pay attention to your father and do not despise your mother		
Ecclesiastes 12.1	-remember God		
Mark 7:10	-honor your parents		
Ephesians 6.1	-obey your parents		
Proverbs 1:8	-pay attention to instructions from your mother and father		

Notes

Building Blocks for Relationships

Workshop Exercise # 5
(Parent)

Directions:
1. Search the selected verses and identify the biblical principles described. In your group session make a list of the principles found (20 minutes)

2. Privately identify the principles you are presently applying in your relationship as a parent. Briefly explain how you are fulfilling each principle. (10 minutes)

3. Identify the principles you are not fulfilling. Describe a brief plan for how you intend to fulfill them. Be prepared to share at your discretion. (10 minutes)

Bible Scripture	Biblical Qualities	Applying	Not Applying
Deuteronomy 6:7	-duty to teach		
Proverbs 22:6	-duty to train		
2 Corinthians 12:14	-provide for		
Ephesians 6:4	-nurture		
I Timothy 3:4	-control over		
Titus 2:4	-give love		
Proverbs 13:24	-to correct		
Proverbs 19:18	-discipline		

Notes

Building Blocks for Relationships

Workshop Exercise # 6
(Friend)

Directions:
1. Search the selected verses and identify the biblical principles described. In your group session make a list of the principles found (20 minutes)

2. Privately identify the principles you are presently applying in your relationship as a friend. Briefly explain how you are fulfilling each principle. (10 minutes)

3. Identify the principles you are not fulfilling. Describe a brief plan for how you intend to fulfill them. Be prepared to share at your discretion. (10 minutes)

Bible Scripture	Biblical Qualities	Applying	Not Applying
Galatians 5:22–23 (list each fruit of the spirit and describe how you produce that fruit in your relationship)	-Fruit of the spirit (Proverbs 17:17 love joy peace long suffering gentleness goodness faith meekness temperance		
Proverbs 18:24	-loyalty		
Proverbs 27:10	-cherish old friendships		
Proverbs 27:17	-a source for refinement		
Ecclesiastes 4:9	-work together		
I Samuel 18:1	-bound together deeply		
2 Corinthians 2:13	-seek after one another		

Notes

Building Blocks for Relationships

Workshop Exercise # 7
(A Man, A Husband)

Directions:
1. Search the selected verses and identify the biblical principles described. In your group session make a list of the principles found (20 minutes)

2. Privately identify the principles you are presently applying in your relationship as a man or a husband. Briefly explain how you are fulfilling each principle. (10 minutes)

3. Identify the principles you are not fulfilling. Describe a brief plan for how you intend to fulfill them. Be prepared to share at your discretion. (10 minutes)

Bible Scripture	Biblical Qualities	Applying	Not Applying
Proverbs 22:2	-all are made equal		
Galatians 3:28	-no distinction in humanity		
Job 32:8	-inspiration and understanding from God		
Genesis 2:24	-separation from everything to be with his wife		
Ecclesiastes 9:9	-live joyfully with wife		
Ephesians 5:25	-love your wife		
I Peter 3:7	-honor your wife		
Deuteronomy 6:7	-to teach the children		
2 Corinthians	-provide for family		
Ephesians 6:4	-nurture the children		
I Timothy 3:4	-control over children		
Proverbs 13:24	-apply correction		

Notes

Bibliography

Bibles:

1. The Holy Bible, Authorized King James Version, World Publishing, Iowa Falls, IA, USA. "Scriptures used by permission"

2. New American Standard Bible, Foundation Publications, Inc., Copyright 1998 by the Lockman Foundation, Anaheim, CA "Scripture taken from the New American Standard Bible ®, Copyright 1960, 1962, 1963, 1968, 1971, 1972, 1973, 1975, 1977, 1995, by The Lockman Foundation. Used by permission. www. Lockman.org

3. New International Version, Bible Soft PC Study Bible® Version 4, Copyright 1998–2003, Bible Soft, Inc.

References:

4. *Young's Analytical Concordance To The Bible*, Robert Young, LL.D., Thomas Nelson Publishers, New York, 1982

5. *A Critical Lexicon and Concordance to The English and Greek New Testament*, Bullinger, Ethelbert W., First Zondervan Printing, Grand Rapids, MI, 1975

6. *The Thompson Chain-Reference Bible*, 5th Ed, B. B. Kirkbride Bible Co., Inc., Indianapolis, IN, USA, 1982

7. *Holman Bible Dictionary*, Butler, Trent C., Gen. Ed., Holman Bible Publishers, Nashville, TN, 1991

Printed in the United States
136304LV00002B/3/P

9 780595 491568